CW01652413

FIRST CERTIFICATE NETWORK

3 LISTENING & SPEAKING

Ken Wilson

Course Consultants

Simon Greenall and Judy Garton-Sprenger

Self-Study Edition with Key

HEINEMANN

Heinemann International
A division of Heinemann Publishers (Oxford) Ltd
Halley Court, Jordan Hill, Oxford OX2 8EJ

OXFORD LONDON EDINBURGH
MADRID ATHENS BOLOGNA PARIS
MELBOURNE SYDNEY AUCKLAND SINGAPORE TOKYO
IBADAN NAIROBI HARARE GABORONE
PORTSMOUTH (NH)

ISBN 0 435 28574 2
Cassettes 0 435 28578 5

First published 1991

ACKNOWLEDGEMENTS

This book is dedicated to Ben Warren.

The author wishes to thank the following: Brian Bowles, Elaine Claxton, David Drysdale, Sheelagh Gilbey, Hazel Imbert, Simon Parrish and Christopher Rowe for their help in the recording. Dede Wilson and other members of Westminster College for their help in piloting the material.

The publishers would like to thank the following people for their help: Katie Head and Nick Kenny.

Cassettes produced by Ken Wilson at Motivation Studios.

We would like to thank the following for permission to reproduce copyright material: Jonathon Cape Ltd, extract from 'The House of the Spirits' by Isabel Allende (p.45); William Heinemann Ltd, 'To Kill a Mocking Bird' by Harper Lee (p.45); William Heinemann Ltd, 'A Question of Upbringing' by Anthony Powell (p.45).

Illustrations by: Kathy Baxendale (p. 2, 26, 29 and 77) and Sue Heape (p. 19, 33 and 61).

Photographs by: AA Picture Library (p.45), Allsport/Bob Martin (p.52 bottom), Bob Thomas Sports Photography (p.52 top), Domino (p.23), Environmental Picture Library (Graham Burns p.19, Robert Brook-centre p.33, V. Miles-right p.33, Martin Bond-left p.33), Fortean Picture Library/ Dima Girenko (p.88), Impact Photos/Roger Perry (p.73), John Leaver (p.63), Kobal Collection/Bob Penn (p.4), Network (Justin Leighton-left, Laurie Sparham-right p.75), Paul Freestone (p.32), Photographer's Picture Library/Sally and Richard Greenhill (p.10, p.17, p.19-centre, p.61-centre, p.80), Quadrant Picture Library (p.46), TRH (p.61), Zefa (p.19-Rossenbach, p.38, p.61-left and right, p.75-Jonas)

Cover design by: Simon Stafford
Designed by: Holdsworth Associates

Printed and bound in Great Britain by:
The Bath Press, Avon, England

91 92 93 94 95 96 10 9 8 7 6 5 4 3 2 1

Contents

Starter unit

This starter unit will introduce you to the style of the activities and exercises in this book.

LISTENING

Each unit in this book has two listening extracts. Before you listen to each one, there will be some **pre-listening activities**. The first extract in this unit is a conversation between a police officer and a woman who owns a shop. The conversation takes place in her shop. Here are your pre-listening activities:

Task 1

Predict what the subject-matter will be Which of the following topics are likely subjects for their conversation?

- the weather
- a recent robbery
- an unpaid tax bill
- the political situation
- the local soccer team

Task 2

What do you expect to hear? Which of the following words and phrases could possibly appear in a conversation between a police officer and a shop owner?

routine enquiry	good value	questions	responsible	robbery
sale price	competition	invitation	attractive	

After you have completed pre-listening activities like these, you will find ideas and exercises designed to be done while listening to the cassette for the first time. For example, you may be asked to listen for some specific information:

Task 3

Listening for a specific purpose Read the following questions and find the answers when you listen to the cassette:

a Was the shop owner expecting a visit from the police officer? How do you know?

b Who was in the shop at the time of the robbery?

Now listen to the cassette and try to answer these questions. Don't worry if you fail to understand every word that you hear. In the examination, you will always hear the extract twice, and you will always get more of the meaning by reading the examination question itself.

For every listening extract in this book, there are further activities to encourage you to listen to the cassette again. Some of these activities are in the style of Paper Four exercises. Here are two examples:

Task 4

Listen to the cassette again and complete the True or False exercise below. (It is important to read the statements in this kind of exercise *before* you listen to the cassette. It will give you an idea of the subject-matter of what you are about to hear.)

		True	False
a	Inspector Black works for the CIA.		
b	Mrs Carter is the owner of the shop.		
c	She was in the shop for less than three hours yesterday.		
d	The people who robbed the bank were arrested.		
e	Mrs Carter is not the shop manager.		
f	The shop manager works at the shop on Fridays.		

Task 5

Look at theses three diagrams. Which is the most accurate indication of the position of the shop and the bank?

1

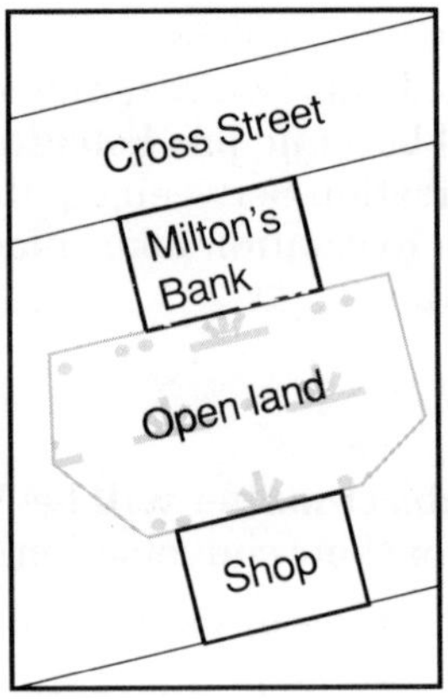

2

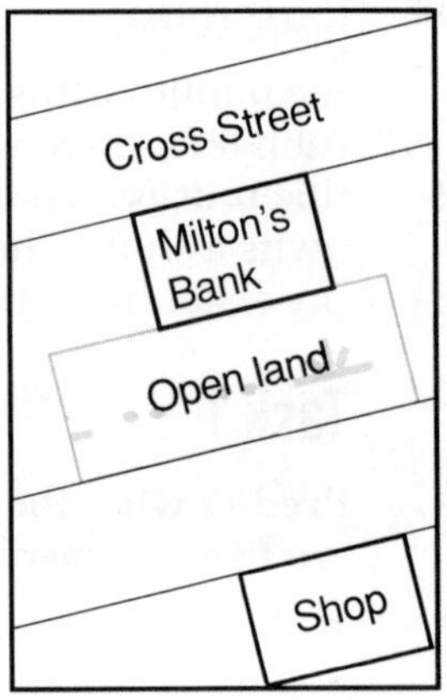

3

After these examination-style exercises, there will be some activities based on a closer examination of the text of the listening extract.

Here are some examples:

Task 6

Intonation practice Look at the extract from the conversation. Will the intonation rise or fall at the end of the questions? Mark ↘ if you think it will rise and ↗ if you think it will fall. Then listen to the cassette again.

Inspector Are you the owner of this shop?
Mrs Carter Yes, I am.
Inspector And were you here yesterday?
Mrs Carter Yes.
Inspector Can you tell me what time you arrived?
Mrs Carter Yes, but why do you want to know?
Inspector Just a routine enquiry, Mrs Carter. What time did you arrive?
Mrs Carter About 9.30.
Inspector And what time did you leave?

Task 7

Words missing
Look at the next part of the conversation. There are some words missing in the written version. Listen and mark ‸ when there is a word missing.

Mrs Carter I stayed until midday.
Inspector I see. You weren't here in the afternoon?
Mrs Carter No. What is this about?
Inspector Was anybody here?
Mrs Carter Inspector, you must tell me why you're asking all these questions.
Inspector There was a robbery at Milton's Bank yesterday. The people left the bank … and disappeared.

Task 8

Sounds practice /æ/ and /ɑː/

The name of the police officer is Black /blæk/ and the name of the shop owner is Carter /kɑːtə/. Here are some more words from the conversation. Some of them include the sound /æ/ and some include the sound /ɑː/. Some of the words don't include either sound. Make three lists.

back	arrived	asking	afternoon	address	contacting
bank	that	pack	anybody	Friday	can (weak form)
man	woman	manager	Parker		

The second extract in this starter unit is about the first manned space flight to the moon. Here are two more pre-listening activities:

Task 9

What do you already know? Make a note of anything you know about the first manned flight to the moon.

- Who were the people involved?
- What nationality were they?
- What was the name of their craft?
- When did it take place?
- Where did they leave from?

Task 10

Make sure you know the meaning With some listening extracts, it is recommended that you know the meaning of certain key words and phrases. Before listening to the piece about the moon, check the meaning of the following:

spacecraft	set foot on	lunar module	orbit	samples
surface	astronauts	mankind	crater	

Task 11

Listening for a specific purpose When you listen to the cassette, listen specifically to the names of the three astronauts and the name of the launching site in Texas. The names are written here, but they are mixed up. Pair them correctly.

Neil Collins
Cape Aldrin
Buzz Kennedy
Michael Armstrong

Task 12

Now listen again and complete the multiple choice exercise below. Read through the questions quickly before you listen. It will give you a good idea of what you will hear.

1 The first manned spacecraft to the moon left
a from Houston.
b on July 21st, 1969.
c from a launching site in Texas.
d four days late.

2 After four days, Apollo 11
a landed on the moon.
b returned to Earth.
c descended to the moon's surface.
d began to orbit the moon.

3 The moon landing took place
a on July 17th, 1969.
b four days after departure.
c in a crater.
d after a long voyage.

4 The two astronauts who landed on the moon
a had surnames beginning with the same letter.
b stayed in the lunar module.
c avoided landing in Apollo.
d were called Neil and Michael.

Task 13

How much can you remember about the moon landing?
Work in pairs. Close your books and tell each other the sequences of events.

Task 14

Extra words Listen to the cassette and read the extract . There are some extra words in the written version. Listen and mark any words that you do not hear.

The journey only lasted for four days. Finally, Apollo 11 went into orbit around the moon.Collins remained alone in the spacecraft, and the other two descended to the moon's surface together in a much smaller craft, the lunar module. After a moment of high drama, when the two astronauts narrowly avoided landing in a deep crater, the lunar module finally reached its destination.

Task 15

Wrong words In the next part, some of the words are wrong. Listen and mark any words that are not what you hear.

So, on July 21st, Armstrong began the first person to set food on the moon. His first works, as he stood on the moon surface, were these: 'That's one small stop for a man, one giant leak for mankind.'

Task 16

Missing endings In the final part of the piece, some of the endings of the words are missing or wrong. Listen and mark any words that are not what you hear.

Armstrong and Aldrin collect sample of dust and rot and took photograph before return to Apollo for the return journal to Earth.

Task 17

Pronunciation practice In British English, two of the astronauts' surnames include the sound /ɒ/ (as in 'lot' or 'wash'). Which ones? In which of the following words from the extract does the same sound occur?

Apollo	one	other	aboard	rock	moment
orbit	voyage	dust	module	four	photographs

Task 18

Discussion Some of the listening texts in the book can lead to a discussion. With this one, you could discuss the following:

- Did the moon astronauts do something of great importance, or was it all a waste of money?
- Why do you think there have been so few visits to the moon?
- Would you want to go on a trip like that?

SPEAKING

The second section of each unit is devoted to the skills you need in Paper Five of the examination, the Interview.

One of the main features in Paper Five is a set of photographs and a series of short reading passages which are connected with them. In the book, we will examine photographs and reading passages and see how we can improve your skills at talking about them. First of all, examine this photograph.

Think about the words you need to use to describe what you see:

in the foreground/in the background

on the left/on the right/in the middle/centre

Now think about the words you need to talk about the *actions* and *emotions* of the people. Remember it is not a problem if you are uncertain about these things. You can express your uncertainty in this way:

They look (nervous/angry)	*They look as if (they've seen a ghost)*
They look like (aliens/yuppies)	*They appear to be (running away/from another planet)*

Nor is it a problem if you cannot find the exact words to describe what you see. There are strategies to help you:

I'm not sure what it's called. *It's a bit like .../It's something like ...*

I don't know how to describe that exactly.

Remember, there's nothing wrong with not knowing how to describe something. Just make sure you have the language to express your uncertainty.

Reading passages

Every unit has at least one photograph in this speaking section. (There are always three in the examination practice sections.) Connected to the photographs, in the main part of the unit as well as the examination section, are a series of short reading passages.

In the interview part of the examination, all you have to do is establish a connection between the reading passages and the photographs. In the unit itself, we try to exploit the material more fully.

Although it is not specifically required by the First Certificate examination, you may be asked to identify the *source* and *subject-matter* of a reading extract. In other words, is it taken from a novel? Or a newspaper? A travel brochure? A letter?

And we may ask you to consider the *intention* of the piece. Why was it written? Is it a piece of criticism? An advertisement? A complaint? And what do you look for to find out these things?

Here's an example exercise. Look at the three extracts below, which all contain the word 'aliens'.

a The latest example of the style is *Aliens*, which will be released in most major cities next week. Sadly, it is not the best of its type that I have seen.

b I am writing to complain about the treatment of a foreign colleague of mine by your immigration officers. She was subjected to very upsetting questioning by an extremely suspicious person. It seems to me as if European Community Citizens are still being treated as aliens.

c *Aliens.* Be prepared to be afraid. Very afraid.

Now answer these questions:

1. Two of the extracts are referring to the film *Aliens*. Which ones? How do you know?
2. One of the two referring to the film is an advertisement. The other is a newspaper review. Which is which?
3. What is the meaning of the word 'aliens' in the extract which does not refer to the film? The extract is taken from a letter. Is it a letter to a newspaper? How do you know?

Role-play

Act out the conversation between the suspicious immigration officer and the innocent visitor.

To act out a situation successfully, you need to think about what each character would say and why. You must also pay attention to how each character would *react* to what the other says. Let's look at each of the two characters in our role-play:

The immigration officer

- Why are you suspicious? Do you think the visitor has a false passport? Or is he/she planning to stay in your country longer than is permitted? Or are the police looking for someone?
- Are you bored? Or tired? Or angry about something? If so, what are you angry about?
- What caused you to be suspicious? The passport? The visitor's appearance? Something he/she said?
- What words and phrases express *suspicion*?

The visitor

- Where are you from? And where are you travelling to?
- What is your first reaction when the immigration officer expresses suspicion? Are you surprised? Confused? Nervous? Angry?
- What words and phrases express *confusion*?
- How can you ask the immigration officer to repeat what he/she has said?

Discussion

Refugees, immigrants and other visitors. Should all countries give residence to anyone who wants to live there? Or is it necessary to control the numbers?

Exam practice

At the end of each unit is an examination practice section, either for Paper Four or Paper Five of the First Certificate. The contents (exercises and instructions) are all in the style of the examination.

The Paper Four examination practice sections consist of four listening extracts with accompanying exercises. In the examination itself, there are only two.

In the Paper Five examination practice sections, there is a page for the 'candidate' and a page for the 'examiner'. Your teacher may want to be the examiner or s/he may want the class to examine each other in pairs. The examiner's page will have instructions about how to exploit the material on the candidate's page.

Now that you have completed this Starter Unit, you should be familiar with the style of this book. In each unit, there are two listening extracts, followed by activities which include the kind of material that you will encounter when you take the First Certificate Paper Four and Paper Five. Here are a few points for you to consider:

About listening

- The Paper Four examination simply consists of two short listening extracts, each of which you hear twice. With each extract, there is one exercise and you are allowed to read it before you hear the cassette.
- It doesn't matter if you don't understand *everything*. You will hear the listening extract twice, and you will always be able to answer most of the questions.
- If you read the question, you will often learn a lot about what you are going to hear.
- Remember to listen to the key words, and don't worry about the ones you don't understand.

About speaking

- The Paper Five examination is *not* a test of your general knowledge. It is not even a test of the number of words that you know in English. It is simply a chance for you to express yourself as well as you can.
- If you don't know the word for something in a photograph, all you have to do is say what it is that you don't know.
- Remember that examiners are not monsters! They are all trained to help you overcome your nervousness and give yourself a chance to do your best.

All in a day's work

LISTENING 1 How do you learn a language?

Task 1

Discuss which of the following you think are important or necessary if you want to learn to speak a foreign language.

- having lessons with a native speaker
- travelling to a country where the language is spoken
- finding friends who speak the language
- having one-to-one lessons
- listening to radio broadcasts in the language
- taking examinations
- reading as much as you can

Task 2

You're going to hear an interview with a language student talking about the methods she uses to improve her English. Her name is Monica Russo. What nationality could she be?

Listen to the cassette. Look at the list of language skills on the right. Tick (✓) the skills she has no trouble with and put a cross (✗) if she finds them difficult. Put this mark (—) if she doesn't refer to them at all.

Now listen again to Monica explaining her unusual way or practising her English in the street. Where is she learning English?

	No problems	Finds difficult
Listening		
Speaking		
Pronunciation		
Grammar		
Reading		
Writing		
Spelling		

Task 3

Read the extract below and re-write it, omitting the repetitions and other aspects of spoken English.

Sometimes it's quite difficult to meet English people and to practise the language … so well the way I practise my English is watching TV most of the time or sometimes I'm just … I'm in the street walking and I just stop people you know in the street plain blond English face looking you know looking face and I just say um I'm sorry er what time is it please you know and then they start saying the time and or maybe you know you appear a bit lost in the street and English people are very helpful and they come to you and they say and can I help you any … anyhow oh yes please! you know I'm really lost and I don't know where this place is and that way you just start a conversation you know it's just a good way of practise … practising the language.

Task 4

Here is another extract from what Monica said. But some words have been omitted in the written version. Indicate (⋏) when you hear something that is not written.

Reading and writing. I … I read quite a lot and I read more in English than Italian now and I've got to start picking up Italian books … um I … I read lots of newspapers you know from the gossipy ones to the intellectual ones. I do like writing er when I've got time, I always keep in touch with friends. I'm quite confident about my writing because I studied quite a lot at school and they've given me a very good basis and I'm very confident in my spelling.

Task 5

Difficult or easy? /ɪ/ or /iː/?

Here is a list of words used by Monica in the interview. Do they contain an /ɪ/ or /iː/ sound?

English	speaking	people	reading	street	listening
please	illogical	middle	TV	skills	irregular

LISTENING 2 Who's in Town?

Task 1

Who's in Town? is the name of a chat show … a light entertainment TV programme where people in the news are interviewed. Which of the following types of people would you expect to see on the programme?

film directors	soap stars	poets
pop stars	novelists	taxi drivers
architects	nurses	typists
actors	politicians	movie stars

Task 2

You are going to hear an interview with a character in a soap opera called *The People Next Door*. Before you listen, make sure you know the meaning of the following words and expressions:

studio	broadcast	make-up department
series	script	character (in a play)
episode	scene	studio set
facade	alarm call	commercial break

Task 3

In the interview, the soap star, Celia Street, talks about her *daily routine*. As you listen make notes in the chart on the right about what she does at the indicated times. Some have been written for you.

4.45 am	*Alarm call*
5.00 am	
5.45 am	*Studio car arrives*
6.00 am	
6.30 am	*Make-up Department*
7.30 am	
8.30 am	

Task 4

Now read the True or False exercise below. Listen to the cassette again and tick (✓) the appropriate column.

	True	False
a Celia Street is the star of a British TV series.		
b The series has been on TV in Britain for three months.		
c They broadcast two episodes of the series every week.		
d The programme is filmed outside a TV studio.		
e Celia plays an immigrant English girl in the series.		
f Celia got the part when she was visiting some Australian musicians.		
g In her free time, she finds out what Australia is really like.		

Task 5

Look at the extract from the conversation below. Mark the words that you expect to be *stressed*, and indicate if you expect the intonation to go up (↗) or down (↘) at the end of each sentence.

Interviewer What do the people who live in the actual street think about all this filming at night?

Celia What do you mean ... the people in the street?

Interviewer The residents of Carey Street, or whatever the real name is.

Celia It isn't a real street.

Interviewer What?

Celia It isn't a real street!

Interviewer Not a real street!

Celia No! I thought everybody knew that!

Interviewer I didn't! I thought it was a real street!

Celia No ... it's a studio set! It's in the car-park behind the TV studio!

Interviewer It must be enormous!

Celia What?

Interviewer The car-park.

Celia Why?

Task 6

Now listen to the extract again and check your answers.

Task 7

Below is Celia's explanation of the character she plays in the series. But there are some extra words in the written version. Listen to the cassette again. Follow the extract below as you listen and underline any words that you don't hear.

I play a young English girl called Elizabeth who has just arrived in the local neighbourhood. Her family has recently emigrated from England and almost everything is very different. She sort of spends most of her time getting things completely wrong because she simply doesn't understand what people are saying to her, or she doesn't understand how the money works. She initially goes to the local high school, which is really very different from the school she originally went to in England.

Task 8

What kind of words are most of the extra ones?

Write down five words or expressions about *routine* that you have heard in this lesson.

SPEAKING Women at work

Task 1

Look at the picture. Make notes of all the things you can see in it, in as much detail as you can. Write something about all of the following:

- the women themselves
- their clothes and appearance
- the work they're doing
- the place where they are
- when the photograph was taken

Divide the photograph into *foreground* and *background* and talk about what is *on the left, on the right, at the front, at the back*, etc.

Remember ... you can say *Some women are working ...*

but it sounds better if you say *There are some women working ...*

Task 2

If you want to express an opinion about, for example, how people are feeling, or what sort of lives they lead, you should try to use expressions like this:

*They **look** tired ...* *They look **as if** they're working too hard ...*

***Maybe** they're tired ... .* *I **imagine/should think/expect/suppose** ...*

Task 3

When you have finished making notes about the photograph, answer the following questions:

a How many people are there in the photograph?
b What are they doing?
c Where are they?
d When do you think the photograph was taken?
e Do the people look happy?
f Do you think they enjoy their work?

Questions **d–f** are asking you to express an opinion. If you are not sure of your answer, or you want to give two opinions, try to use the following expressions:

I don't know for sure …
I'm not sure but I think …
This is only a guess, but …
It's hard to say from the photo …

Task 4

Read the three passages below and then answer the questions.

a On average, I work a twelve-hour-day … and that's at least six days a week. I would estimate that I spend more time in front of the screen than I do anywhere else … maybe seven hours a day. That's more time than I spend in bed!

b She likes the people she works with, but she doesn't like the work. It is quite monotonous and very tiring. At the end of each working day, she has no energy left at all, and spends the evening in front of the television.

c Depending on my work-shift, I'm on call for between eight and twelve hours a day. It's longer during the day but the nights are the hardest. We play cards all the time between calls, but it's hard to stay awake. Things are much better now that the station has satellite TV. We watch the sports channel almost all the time.

Which of the following people do you think the three passages refer to?

- a firefighter
- an airline pilot
- a factory worker
- a computer operator
- an autograph hunter
- a film director

Task 5

Which words in the three passages about people express the idea of *routine*?

Task 6

Role-play Choose one of the three occupations that are being described in the three reading passages. Act out the role of a person working in this job. Decide whether or not the work gives you *job satisfaction*. With another student, act out an interview, giving your reasons why you are or are not satisfied.

Task 7

Discussion Discuss the daily or weekly routine of the three people listed in Task 4 who were *not* described in the reading passages.

Exam practice: paper 4 LISTENING COMPREHENSION

FIRST PART

Match the films listed below with the cinemas where they are playing.
Indicate the correct film by its letter only.

A *Rainman*
B *Drowning by Numbers*
C *Some Like it Hot*
D *John Ford Western*
E *Baghdad Cafe*

<table>
<tr><th>Odeon</th><th>One</th><th>Two</th><th>Three</th><th>Four</th><th>Five</th></tr>
<tr><td>Monday–Thursday</td><td></td><td rowspan="2">E</td><td rowspan="2">D</td><td></td><td rowspan="2">C</td></tr>
<tr><td>Friday–Sunday</td><td>B</td><td>A</td></tr>
<tr><td>Late–night
Friday + Saturday</td><td></td><td></td><td></td><td>B</td><td></td></tr>
</table>

SECOND PART

Fill in the transport questionnaire. Tick (✓) the appropriate answers.

PUBLIC TRANSPORT SURVEY

a Public transport used
- ☐ every weekday
- ☐ regularly at weekends
- ☐ occasionally at weekends
- ☐ rarely at weekends

b Purpose of weekday travel
☐ work ☐ leisure ☐ other

c Destination
☐ central area ☐ suburban area

d Time of morning journey
☐ before 8.00 ☐ 8.00–8.15 ☐ 8.15–8.30
☐ 8.30–8.45 ☐ 8.45–9.00 ☐ After 9.00

e Length of morning journey
☐ Less than 20 minutes ☐ More than 20 minutes

f Time of evening journey
☐ 4.30–5.00 ☐ 5.00–5.30 ☐ 5.30–6.00

g Season ticket?
☐ Yes ☐ No

THIRD PART

For questions **1–6** tick (✓) whether the statements are true or false.

		True	False
1	Human and pet behaviour are not similar.		
2	Dogs wag their tails because they love their owners		
3	When owners shout at their dogs, the dogs feel guilty.		
4	Dogs behave better because they fear punishment.		
5	Cats are far more intelligent than dogs.		
6	The relatives of dogs and cats in the wild behave in a similar fashion to each other.		

FOURTH PART

For questions **7–12** tick (✓) one of boxes, **A**, **B**, **C**, or **D**.

7 Computers can easily solve mathematical problems that

A	take months to set.	**A**	
B	humans can do in seconds.	**B**	
C	would take a person a very long time.	**C**	
D	mathematicians can't understand.	**D**	

8 Computers are simply machines

A	with three basic abilities.	**A**	
B	that can only store information.	**B**	
C	that turn information into data.	**C**	
D	that retrieve information.	**D**	

9 Data is another word for

A	numbers.	**A**	
B	words.	**B**	
C	computers.	**C**	
D	information.	**D**	

10 The input unit of a computer

A	is a typewriter.	**A**	
B	stores information.	**B**	
C	is the memory.	**C**	
D	can be a keyboard.	**D**	

11 The central processing unit displays the results

A	only on a printer.	**A**	
B	on a television set.	**B**	
C	on a screen or printer.	**C**	
D	on a keyboard.	**D**	

12 'Visual Display Unit' is the name given to

A	the printer.	**A**	
B	the screen.	**B**	
C	the keyboard.	**C**	
D	the computer.	**D**	

The world around us

LISTENING 1 Getting a bank loan

Task 1

On the cassette, you are going to hear a telephone conversation between a bank employee and someone who wishes to borrow money from the bank. Before you listen, look at the list of words below. Which ones would you expect to hear?

account	job	married	criminal
loan	reason	impossible	bicycle
children	swim	details	earn
smoker	computer	famous	important

Task 2

Look at the Loan Application Form below. Look at the details that the bank employee has to write down. Make a note of the questions that need to be asked to get this information. Do this **before** you listen to the tape.

Task 3

Look at the True or False exercise below. Read it before you listen to the cassette and then tick (✓) the appropriate box as you listen.

	True	False
a Peter Sharp is applying for employment.		
b This is the first time he has contacted the bank.		
c He works at a computer factory.		
d He's been working there for a month.		
e Mr Sharp is married with no children.		
f He lives in rented accommodation.		
g The bank wants to know if he smokes.		

Task 4

Now complete the form with Mr Sharp's answers.

LOAN APPLICATION FORM

Name *Peter Sharp*

Address *27 Petley Lane*

Occupation *Production Controller*

How long in this employment for? Temporary ☐ Permanent ☐ Trial ☐

Married Yes ☐ No ☐ **Children** Yes ☐ No ☐

Accommodation House ☐ Flat ☐ Other ☐ Rented ☐ Owned ☐

Task 5

Below is an extract from the conversation. But there are some changes from the original. Some words are missing and some have been changed. Listen to the cassette and note the changes. Mark the words that are missing like this (‸) and underline any words that are different.

Archer What do you do, Mr Sharp?

Sharp I'm production control at a computer assembly plan.

Archer And how much do you learn?

Sharp About six hundred a month, after tasks.

Archer How long have you been walking at the plan, Mr Sharp?

Sharp A week.

Archer Is it a permanent partition?

Sharp I'm on a month try. Depends on that, I may gate a permanent chop.

Task 6

/tʃ/ or /ʃ/?

Put the following words from the cassette in the correct list: Archer /ɑːtʃə/ or Sharp /ʃɑːp/.

Chelsea	**s**ure	posi**ti**on	fu**t**ure
produc**ti**on	**sh**op	**ch**ildren	**sh**all

LISTENING 2 Blandsmere Shopping Centre

Task 1

On the cassette, you are going to hear a radio report about a shopping centre in South London. Which of the following would you expect to find in a modern shopping centre?

a sauna	a supermarket	a fish and chip shop
a bookshop	a laundry	a museum
a creche	a swimming pool	a restaurant

Task 2

Below on the left are some of the words and phrases that you will hear on the cassette. Find a word or expression from the column on the right that could mean the same thing.

facilities	suggest
huge	small meals
snacks	covered
encased	very large
recommend	outside
in the open air	services

Task 3

Look at the multiple choice questions below. Read them quickly before you listen to the cassette. You will get an idea of what to expect when you listen. Now listen to the cassette and choose the correct answer.

1 The Blandsmere Shopping Centre
- **a** has been recently built.
- **b** stands in the centre of the city.
- **c** is a complex place.
- **d** is located in the middle of a restaurant.

2 Tessmans Supermarket is
- **a** to the north of the square.
- **b** on the north side of the complex.
- **c** in the middle of the gound floor.
- **d** the biggest one in the complex.

3 There are smaller shops
- **a** to the right of the supermarket.
- **b** selling records, toys, etc.
- **c** in the middle of the square.
- **d** in the supermarket.

4 Marstons Shoe Shop is
- **a** near the restaurant.
- **b** the biggest shop in the complex.
- **c** on the second floor.
- **d** next to the way in.

5 The restaurant
- **a** is downstairs in the basement.
- **b** forms a circle in the middle.
- **c** is below the kitchen.
- **d** goes round.

Task 4

Look at the diagrams. They represent the ground floor and the upper floor of the new Blandsmere Shopping Centre. Listen to the cassette again and mark in where each of the shops and other facilities are.

To help you, the names of some of them have already been filled in, and the ones that you have to locate are listed below.

Locate the following:
Tessmanns Supermarket
wholefood delicatessen
computer shop
furniture store
record store
toyshop
gift shop
flower shop
central restaurant
sports complex
motel

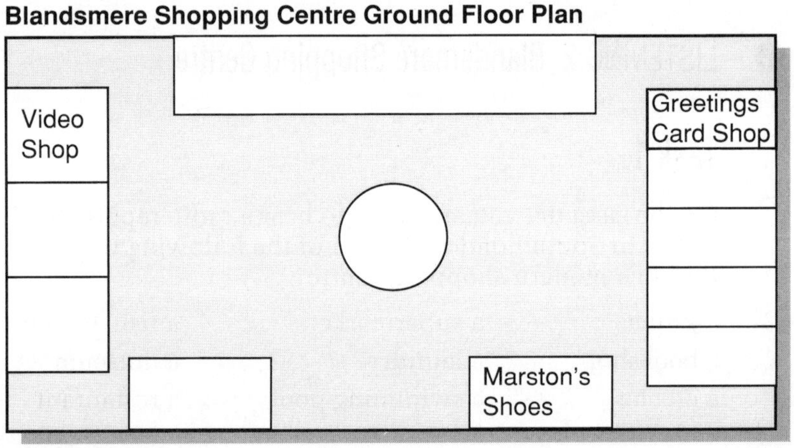

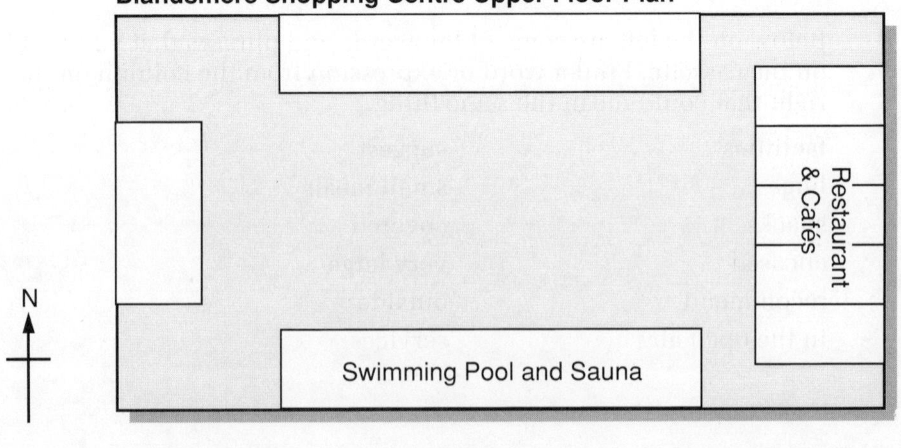

Task 5

Listen to the cassette again, following the first part of the radio report below as you listen. Some of the words on the cassette are missing from the written version. Indicate where there is a word missing (^).

I'm standing in the middle of the ground floor of the Blandsmere Shopping Centre in Croydon, about fifteen miles from London. It's a huge indoor complex, with an extraordinary variety of shops and a large restaurant here in the middle.

In front of me, I can see Tessmann's Supermaket, the biggest I've ever seen. That takes up the north side of the square. On my left, on the west side of the square, there are shops … a video market and a furniture store. On my right are a series of smaller shops. I can see a greetings shop, next to that a record store … and more shops selling toys and flowers.

SPEAKING Lifestyles

Task 1

Look at the two photographs on this page and discuss them with other students. Describe the women and children in them. Talk about the kind of life they may lead.

Task 2

If you want to express your views about *lifestyles*, you should think of things to say about the following:

- where they live
- what they do for a living
- what they own
- where they shop and what they buy
- what they do in their spare time
- what kind of people they know
- their ambitions
- what influences them

Task 3

Read the three passages below.

a Blanche never rose before eleven. Her maid, Elena, knew that she should never even open the curtains of nearby rooms in case sunlight leaked under the door of Blanche's pink-walled bedroom. Elena's husband Mario was Blanche's gardener. He was not to use the electric mower before midday. While Blanche slept, so did the house.

b It seems ages since I last saw you—it was the day before I left for the States, wasn't it? So much has happened, and so much is different. I'm living on the ninth floor of an apartment block overlooking the beach at Sausalito. The view is stunning, or at least it is when there's no smog. I only work afternoons at the clinic, which means I can spend mornings with Alice.

c CAN YOU HELP? Helen is living with her three children in one room. There are hundreds of families like this who need help with clothing, furniture and heating. If you can offer anything, call FAMILIES IN CRISIS.

The passages come from one of the following sources. Which one? And how do you know?

- a short story
- a diary
- an advertisement
- a letter
- an instruction leaflet
- a telephone conversation

Task 4

Two of the passages relate to the photographs. Which ones?

Task 5

Which expressions from the three reading passages describe *routine*?

Task 6

Role-play Read the passage above about Blanche and the maid. Act out the first conversation of the day between them. Before you do this, think about the following:

- Who is Blanche? What kind of person is she? She is obviously rich, but where did her wealth come from? What do you think she would be like as an employer?
- Who are Elena and Mario? Where are they from? Why are they working for Blanche? Do you think they enjoy working there?

Exam practice: paper 5 INTERVIEW

PERSON A

SECTION 1

1

2

3

a The view from the house is splendid. On the other side of the bridge, there's a cluster of shops and restaurants in front of a small marina.

b The place is enormous and the streets are always full of people. Living in such a huge place can be very tense, but also very stimulating.

c It's a very peaceful place where nothing much happens. It can be very cold because the wind is much stronger when it comes straight off the sea.

SECTION 2

1 a 'If you live in a remote place, you spend all your time wondering what's going on in the real world.'

b 'More and more people are finding that the quality of their lives improves when they move away from large cities.'

2 'We moved here for some peace and quiet'

3
- a mountain village
- a city centre hotel
- a lighthouse
- an apartment with three other people
- a house with your parents and other relatives

PERSON B

SECTION 1

Photographs Ask your partner to study the three photographs. Open a discussion using these suggestions:

Describe/compare
- the locations
- the age of the buildings
- the people

Discuss
- why people live in big cities
- the attraction of living on the coast
- why people like living near rivers

If you are working with a group, encourage an individual to start a discussion. Invite other students to answer.

Passages Ask your partner or the group to read the three passages and to link the themes of the passages and the photographs. Invite comments on where the extracts may have been taken from.

SECTION 2

Now choose one of the following activities:

1 **Discussion** Discuss one of the following topics:

a 'If you live in a remote place, you spend all your time wondering what's going on in the real world.'

Prompts
- We need the stimulation of lots of people around us.
- Cinemas, theatres and art galleries are as important as fresh air and open spaces.
- City inhabitants are happy for different reasons.

b 'More and more people are finding that the quality of their lives improves when they move away from large cities.'

Prompts
- People have more time and space away from big cities.
- Life is healthier away from factories and traffic.
- Some people are stimulated by living in the country but others aren't.

2 **Activity 1** Tell your partner or the group to look at the cartoon on their page. Invite comments about it and then ask:
- Why do you think the woman moved to the cottage?
- Do you think the motorway was there when she first moved there?
- How has the motorway changed her life?

3 **Activity 2** Tell your partner or the group to read the list of locations on their page. Ask them to choose their ideal place to live and give reasons.
- a mountain village
- a city centre hotel
- a lighthouse
- an apartment with three other people
- a house with your parents and other relatives

3 Expressing likes, dislikes, preferences and opinions

Each to his own

LISTENING 1 Horror films

Task 1

Below is a list of verbs used to express 'liking' and 'disliking'. Which ones would be appropriate when talking about the types of film that you like?

love	admire	hate	can't stand
in love	desire	despise	can't bear
enjoy	fond of	loathe	fancy

Task 2

Before you listen to the cassette, make sure you know the meaning of the following words and expressions:

the silent era	special effects	science fiction
low budget	Gothic	B-movies
genre	Dracula	

Task 3

Now listen to John talking about why he likes horror movies. He refers to a number of actors, writers and directors. They are listed below. Do you recognise any of the names? Listen to the cassette and write (A) actor, (W) writer or (D) director next to their names.

Christopher Lee	Roger Corman	Peter Cushing
Vincent Price	Bela Lugosi	Jack Nicholson
Peter Lorre	Edgar Allan Poe	Boris Karloff

Task 4

Now read the True or False exercise below. Listen to the cassette again and tick (✓) the appropriate column.

	True	False
a The first horror film was made in the nineteenth century.		
b Hammer horror films began in the 1940s.		
c Roger Corman made low-budget Dracula films.		
d Jack Nicholson has appeared in a large number of horror films.		
e *The Raven* was directed by Edgar Allan Poe.		

Task 5

In the extract below, there are some extra words in the written version that are not in the spoken version. Listen to the extract and cross out the words you don't hear.

They all use this idea of a house on a hill in a storm or in a dark forest or somewhere out of the way where you are completely isolated. I think that's why Psycho is so totally memorable as well because it's an isolated place and the image of the mysterious house on the hill. People can imagine themselves being there and actually being in that situation. They never have anything like telephones and the electricity never works and there's always going to be a cellar. It's the darkness that's in all of us.

Task 6

'It's the darkness that's in all of us.' This is John's explanation of the fascination of horror films. Do you agree with him? Do you like horror films, or do you find them terrifying? Or, even worse, boring?

LISTENING 2 Advertising

Task 1

On the cassette, you are going to hear seven radio advertisements. Below are the names of the products and services being advertised. What kind of things do you think they are?

Kattomilk	Sunday Post	Bantam Runners	Carcover
Securex	Benson's	Seafresh	

Now listen to the cassette. Were you right?

Task 2

Listen to the advertisements again and answer the multiple choice definitions below. If you read through the definitions quickly before you hear the tape, you will have a good idea of which answer you are going to choose.

1 The first product is
- **a** not to be consumed by animals.
- **b** a chocolate drink.
- **c** liquid nourishment for cats.
- **d** a vitamin drink for children.

2 Securex is the name of
- **a** a kind of door.
- **b** a window frame.
- **c** a make of lock.
- **d** a security company.

3 The product Seafresh is a kind of
- **a** washing powder.
- **b** shampoo.
- **c** processed fish.
- **d** deodorant.

4 Carcover is
- **a** a kind of life insurance.
- **b** a car-cleaner.
- **c** a car protection plan.
- **d** something to cover your car.

5 Benson's is probably a
- **a** manufacturer of carpets and curtains.
- **b** furniture removal company.
- **c** make of furniture.
- **d** department store.

6 'Bantam Runners' is the name of
- **a** a team of marathon runners.
- **b** a type of footwear.
- **c** a kind of chicken.
- **d** a police force.

Task 3

Below are two of the advertisements. But there are some extra words which are not on the cassette. Put a line through any words that you don't hear.

No one likes to come home late and find that their house has been ransacked. It's even worse when you know they got in only because your doors and windows weren't securely locked. Do the really sensible thing … fit Securex locks to all your doors and windows. Securex locks really protect your house from unwelcome visitors. So … fit Securex … before you find it's too late.

Sally Richards talks about the *Sunday Post*:

'I really love it … it's got absolutely everything I could possibly want in a Sunday newspaper. I think I'd rather read the *Sunday Post* than almost anything else. Yes … you could almost say I prefer the *Sunday Post*!'

Sally Richards usually reads the *Sunday Post*. Read it on Sunday and you could possibly win an exciting holiday for two in sunny Madagascar. The *Sunday Post*. Try to read it.

Task 4

/s/ or /z/?

All the words below are on the cassette. Which sound do they end with: /s/ or /z/? Can you establish any rules for the pronunciation of these sounds?

thinks	pairs	else	locks	likes	business
clothes	needs	doors	Richards	housewives	curtains
peace	sales	vitamins	carpets		

Task 5

Work in groups. Choose one of the products below and write your own radio advertisement.

- Happy Highland Scotch Whisky
- Charlie's Cut-Price Computer Store
- Ritz … the magazine for the very rich
- Delirium Perfume for women
- Brazilco Coffee

Read your advertisement to the other groups.

2

SPEAKING Car advertising

1

Task 1

Look at the two advertisements for cars on this page. They are obviously aimed at different kinds of people. Describe the people who may be attracted by these advertisements.

Task 2

Advertising appeals to people in many different ways. What are the advertisements on the previous page saying about the product? Which of the following words would you use to describe each of the cars?

- economical
- comfortable
- luxurious
- fast
- inexpensive
- exclusive
- small
- durable
- environment-friendly

Task 3

Which of the two cars appeals to you more? Or do you prefer cars that are different from both of them? Or are you against the use of cars at all? Talk about your *likes*, *dislikes* and *preferences*. Some of the words and expressions in Task 1 at the beginning of this unit may be useful and the following expressions may also be helpful:

I'd rather have …
I'd prefer …
I'd be much happier with …
I'm not keen on …
It isn't my kind of …

Task 4

Read the three passages below.

a Comfortable, quiet, easy to drive … the Newton Carnival is the car you need for the 1990s. We think it's the best car we've ever built. We're sure you'll agree.

b This week, I tested the Newton Carnival. It's very comfortable, quiet and easy to drive … just like it says in the advertising. However, for such a big car, it's not very powerful. Speaking personally, I would have preferred less comfort and more power. Next week, I'll be looking at a new Japanese sports car.

c I'm writing to say what I think about your new car, the Newton Carnival. I bought one three months ago and, by and large, I'm very satisfied with it. In my opinion, however, it's a little under-powered.

Task 5

Where are the extracts taken from and how do you know? Choose from this list.

- an advertisement
- a letter to a newspaper
- a car maintenance book
- a letter to the manufacturer
- a newspaper article

Which words tell you that an opinion is being expressed?

Task 6

Role-play (in pairs)

STUDENT A

You are a researcher. You have to stop people in the street and ask them their opinions and preferences about *TV car advertising*. Use the questionnaire on this page. Don't forget to attract the attention of the passer-by first.

STUDENT B

You are stopped in the street by a researcher who wants to know your opinion about TV car advertising. The researcher's questionnaire is on this page. Give your opinions, if you have any. Use the expressions in Task 3 if they are useful.

QUESTIONNAIRE

1 Do you own a car? Yes ☐ No ☐

2 What qualities do you look for in a car?

comfort ☐ reliability ☐
good design ☐ low petrol consumption ☐
high speed ☐ other ☐

3 Do you watch TV car advertising? Yes ☐ No ☐

4 Do you think it is realistic ☐ or unrealistic? ☐

Exam practice: paper 4 LISTENING COMPREHENSION

FIRST PART

Tick (✓) the six facilities that are available at the Kingsland Fitness Centre.

- sauna
- out-door classes
- swimming pool
- running track
- gymnasium
- vegetarian restaurant
- massage
- personal training programme
- light and airy studios
- hairdressing

SECOND PART

Fill in the number of coupons and amounts of cash required for the following petrol station gifts.

		Coupons	Coupons plus cash
1	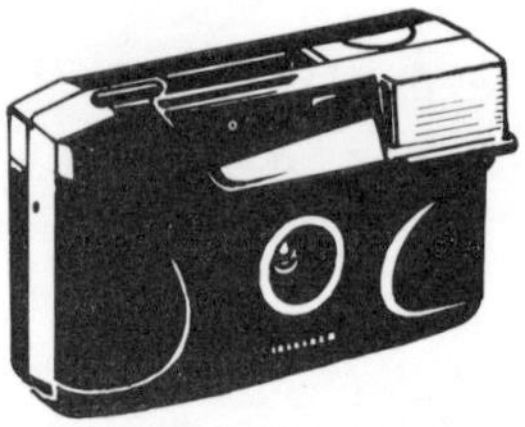		
2	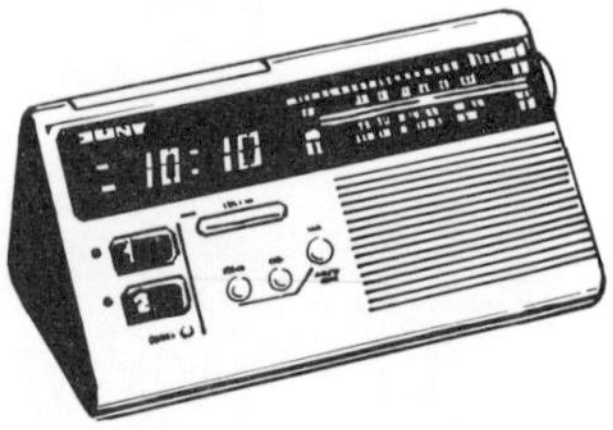		
3			
4	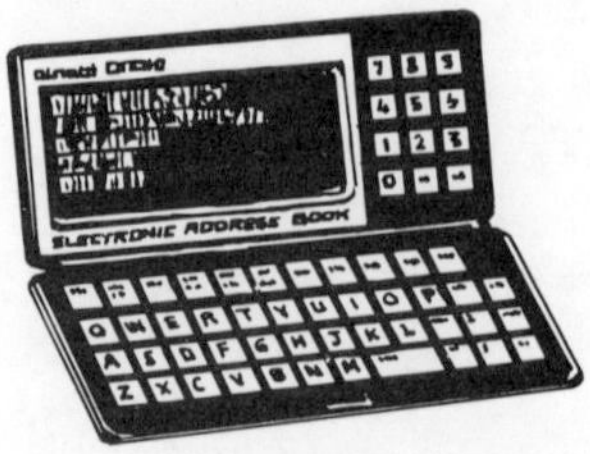		
5			
6	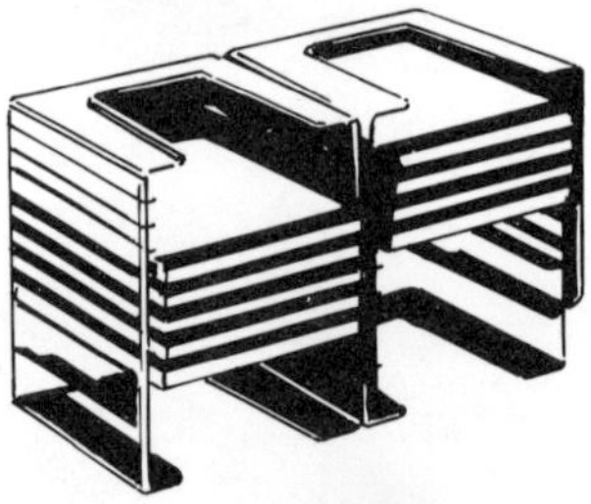		
7			

THIRD PART

For questions **8–13**, tick (✓) one of the boxes **A**, **B**, **C** or **D**.

8 The Van Gogh painting was bought by

A an anonymous agent.
B a doctor.
C an unknown Japanese person.
D an auctioneer.

A	
B	
C	
D	

9 The agent was instructed to

A accept any price for the painting.
B pay what he had to.
C offer a ridiculous price.
D remain anonymous.

A	
B	
C	
D	

10 Paintings by Van Gogh and others are now

A in heavy demand by private collectors.
B disappearing from private collections.
C regularly seen in private collections.
D not left in private collections.

A	
B	
C	
D	

11 Anyone who possesses a Van Gogh or Monet

A will be tempted to sell it.
B loves it a great deal.
C will only accept offers of 50 million dollars.
D will probably put it in the attic.

A	
B	
C	
D	

12 Californian art galleries have been told to

A buy more paintings than New York galleries.
B make their galleries worth more than New York galleries.
C improve the quality of their collections.
D only spend what is necessary.

A	
B	
C	
D	

13 The Californian collection will soon be

A much more valuable than East Coast collections.
B much more expensive than East Coast collections.
C impossible to buy.
D on the West Coast.

A	
B	
C	
D	

FOURTH PART

Put a tick (✓) if the three teenagers like the songs and a cross (✗) if they don't like them.

	Rob	**Anna**	**Steve**
Penny Lane (*The Beatles*)			
Sympathy for the Devil (*The Rolling Stones*)			
Pinball Wizard (*The Who*)			

4 Expressing comparison and contrast

Everything under the sun

LISTENING 1 A pretty normal day

Task 1

Look at the weather symbols below. What do they represent?

Task 2

Match the weather conditions below with the symbols above. There is one which does not have a symbol. Which one is it?

sunny	bright/sunny intervals	light winds	foggy
rain	cloudy	strong winds	thunderstorms

Task 3

Listen to the weather forecast on the cassette. Look at the geographical divisions below and using the symbols above make a note of the expected weather at 6 am and midday. Some of the answers have already been written in to help you.

	6 am	**Midday**
Northern Ireland and Scotland		12°C 
Wales and Northern England	10–12°C 	
South West and Central England		
South East England and East Anglia	fog 12°C 	

Now listen again and check your answers.

Task 4

Look at the map of Great Britain and Ireland. Read the True or False exercise below and listen to the cassette again. Decide which of the general statements about the weather are true or false on the basis of the weather forecast. Tick (✓) the appropriate column.

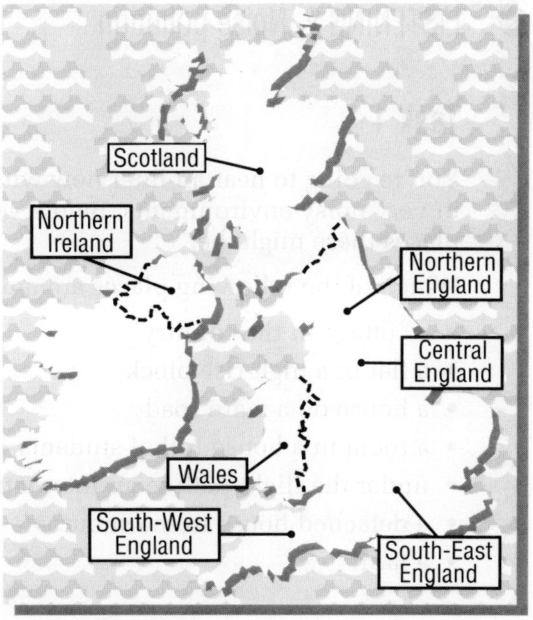

	True	False
a Northern Ireland and Scotland will be the warmest places in Britain.		
b The North of England will get the most rain.		
c The coldest winds will come from the East.		
d The South West will get warmer winds in the early morning.		
e In all areas, the weather will be a little changeable.		

Task 5

/ɔː/ or not?

The vowel sound which makes the word 'or' is /ɔː/. Read the extract from the cassette below and mark any words which include this sound.

Here is the weather forecast for Great Britain and Northern Ireland for tomorrow, Tuesday the fourth of August. First of all, the forecast for six o'clock in the morning.

In Northern Ireland and Scotland, it will be cloudy with occasional showers. Winds will be light and from the north east and there will be mist in sheltered areas. Temperatures will be around six Celsius.

In Wales and Northern England, it will be cloudy with more showers and occasional bright intervals. Winds will be from the south west and temperatures will be higher than the seasonal average at around ten to twelve Celsius.

Task 6

Read the extract from the weather forecast below and underline all the words that you expect to be stressed.

By midday tomorrow, the picture will be quite different. Northern Ireland and Scotland will be mainly sunny with temperatures of twelve degrees Celsius, although a strong east wind will make it seem cooler. Wales and Northern England will experience much heavier rain and cooler temperatures than the rest of the country, with much stronger winds from the south east.

In South West and Central England, the wet and windy start will give way to much warmer weather due to a warm breeze coming from the south east, with occasional bright spells and sunshine. In the South East and East Anglia, expect occasional thunderstorms and heavy rain. Temperatures in this area will be about average.

All in all, a pretty normal day for the weather.

Now listen to the cassette again to check your answers.

LISTENING 2 Noise pollution

Task 1

You're going to hear an interview with someone who lives and works in very noisy environments. Before you listen, think about the possible places these might be.

Which of the following places are most likely to be noisy places to *live*?

- a cottage in the country
- a flat in a high-rise block
- a house on a main road
- a room in a house full of students
- under the flight path to an international airport
- a detached house in the suburbs
- a farm

Task 2

Which of the following places are most likely to be noisy places to *work*?

- a hospital
- a car factory
- a bookshop
- a car-park
- a post office
- a warehouse
- a garage
- a laundry
- a library
- a coalmine
- a school
- a park
- a building site
- a discotheque

Task 3

Before you listen to the cassette, quickly read the statements in the True or False exercise below. Then listen to the cassette and tick (✓) the appropriate box.

		True	False
a	Experts believe noise and stress are related.		
b	Ann's first accommodation was on a busy road.		
c	Things got worse after the local authority banned trucks at night.		
d	Ann then moved to a quieter flat.		
e	Her new neighbours continued making noise after the police left.		
f	She found it quite easy to change her job.		
g	Her second job was in a car factory.		
h	Her stress problem eased after she left the laundry.		

Task 4

Listen to the cassette again and look at the words and expressions listed below. From the context, which of the suggested meanings is most appropriate?

1 lousy
- **a** very low
- **b** expensive
- **c** terrible

2 shirty
- **a** depressed
- **b** annoyed
- **c** anxious

3 worse off
- **a** getting less money
- **b** more unwell
- **c** more unhappy

4 perked up
- **a** received more money
- **b** felt better
- **c** insisted

5 tiptoe
- **a** walk very quietly
- **b** speak very quietly
- **c** dance very quietly

Task 5

Listen to the cassette again while following the extract below. Some of the *endings* of the words are missing. Mark the text where you hear an omission, using this symbol ⋏.

Interviewer Today we focus on the problem of noise, noise at home and noise at work. Medical expert agree that there are definite link between noise and stress level … the noisy the environment, the more stress you are like to experience. And it's even worse when a person is force to live and work in noise environment. This seem to have been the problem for Ann Dickinson.

Ann … the first place I live in when I move here was real lousy. It was on a main road … I was used to living out in the country. There were lorry passing by the front door all day and all night. Then the local council put a ban on truck using that road during the night, so thing got marginal better and I got a bit more sleep. But then I decide to move and thing got much worse …

Task 6

Noise, at home, at school, at work or in the street, is one of the most serious environmental problems of modern city life. Do you have to put up with a lot of noise? What can be done to reduce this problem?

SPEAKING Environmentally-friendly

1

Task 1

Talk about the three photographs on this page. What is the difference between the two items in each photograph?

Task 2

Before you read the three passages below, make sure you know the meaning of these words and expressions.

bio-degradable	recycle	ozone-friendly
canister	aerosol	CFCs
ozone layer	chemical process	

Task 3

Now read the passages. The type of product has been deleted. What kind of products are being discussed?

a So … the answer is simple. Buy (…) in bottles, not in cartons. The cartons are not bio-degradable and it is impossible to recycle them. Make sure you return the (…) bottles to your local shop or dairy.

b Smiths have introduced a new ozone-friendly (…). It comes in the usual style of canister, but it is not an aerosol, contains no CFCs and will cause no damage to the ozone layer. The (…) comes out more slowly, but your hair looks exactly the same.

c White recycled (…) is not as 'green' as it seems. (…) which is recycled from old newspapers, for example, should be grey, not white. It turns white only after an extra chemical process which causes unnecessary water pollution when the chemicals are finally released into the nearest river.

2

3

Task 4

None of the passages is an advertisement. Each one has a different purpose. One is a piece of advice, one is a news item and the other is critical of a product. Which is which and which words indicate the purpose?

Task 5

Discussion A lot of normal household products are suddenly becoming environmentally-friendly. Manufacturers are trying to make products which cause less pollution to the air and the sea and less damage to the environment in other ways.

Tell other students about any examples of this in your country.

Exam practice: paper 5 INTERVIEW

PERSON A

SECTION 1

2

1

3

a As soon as we arrived, we turned round and left. The place was covered in litter. You would think that people who travel all the way to the beach would have more sense.

b They serve food in plastic containers before the match and there's nowhere to put the litter. You can't blame the crowd.

c I don't think they collect the rubbish as often as they used to. Those bags have been sitting there for about five days.

SECTION 2

1 'It's the park attendant from the place we had our picnic yesterday'

2
- an old car
- a metal bed
- a wooden chest of drawers
- a refrigerator
- a crate of empty bottles

PERSON B

SECTION 1

Photographs Ask your partner to study the three photographs in Section 1. Open a discussion using these suggestions:

Describe/compare

- the locations
- the type of litter

Discuss

- how to educate people about litter
- the dangers of litter
- how facilities could be improved

If you are working with a group, encourage an individual to start a discussion. Invite other students to answer.

Passages Ask your partner or the group to read the three passages and to link the themes of the passages and the photographs. Invite comments on where the extracts may have been taken from.

SECTION 2

Now choose one of the following activities:

1 **Discussion** Tell your partner or the group to look at the cartoon on their page and invite their reactions to it.

Prompts

- Why do you think the park attendant is putting rubbish in the garden?
- Is he justified in what he is doing?
- What would you do if this happened to you?

2 **Activity 1** Tell your partner or the group to read the list of items. They have all been found on a rubbish dump. Ask for suggestions about how these items could be recycled.

- an old car
- a metal bed
- a wooden chest of drawers
- a refrigerator
- a crate of empty bottles

3 **Activity 2** Tell your partner or the group to imagine that they have been chosen to solve the litter problem in their town. How would they do it?

Discuss and decide

- how to promote an anti-litter campaign.
- who to speak to.
- where to advertise.
- what positive suggestions you can make.

5 Describing experience and skills

Working and learning

LISTENING 1 The International Jobline

Task 1

On the cassette, you are going to hear a recorded telephone message from an employment agency called International Jobline. The telephone message gives callers up-to-date information about available jobs in other countries. All the jobs are for international companies and require some ability with languages. Which of the following areas of work would you expect them to have information about?

farming	forestry	fishing	medicine	Merchant Navy
accountancy	Armed Services	publishing	oil exploration	television
marketing	tourism	fashion	financial services	

Task 2

Before you listen to the cassette, make sure you understand the meaning of the following words and expressions about *work*.

specialising	preference	position	freelance
starting salary	applicants	experience	
simultaneous translation	hold interviews	full-time	
removal expenses	starting salary	fee	

Task 3

All the jobs on the International Jobline involve languages. Listen to the cassette and fill in the chart. Some of it has been filled in already.

Position	Location	Languages required	Salary
1	*Paris*	*French, English*	*Ffr*
2 *Interpreter*			*Bfr*
3			*fees*

Task 4

Look at the extract from the International Jobline below. The answers to position 2 in Task 3 have been omitted. First, fill in the gaps using the information you heard on the cassette and then mark the words that you expect to be unstressed.

The second job we are offering today is based at the _____ _____ _____ in _____. It's for an _____ who can speak _____, _____ and Dutch and who has experience of simultaneous translation work. The starting salary is _____ per month. All reasonable removal expenses will be paid and assistance will be given in finding accommodation in _____.

Now listen again to see if you were right.

Task 5

This lesson is about *work* /wɜːk/. Which of the following words from the cassette include the sound /ɜː/? (Do not confuse the long sound /ɜː/ with the short sound /ə/ as in wat*er*.)

number	personal	service	successful	interpreters	Brussels
first	Dutch	working	third	company	someone

LISTENING 2 Is education a right or a luxury?

Task 1

You are going to hear someone talking about his education at primary and secondary school. What age do you think he will be talking about?

Which of the following words would you expect to hear in a conversation about education?

enjoyed	delayed	primary	private	college	factory
decided	married	comprehensive	national	farm	sacrifice
increased	dominated	superior	compulsory	institute	academic

Task 2

Now listen to the cassette and tick (✓) the words in the list above that you hear.

Task 3

Which, out of the four options below, is the correct sequence of schooling that Tony received?

1 a primary school **b** infant school **c** secondary school
2 a national school **b** secondary school **c** St Condletts College
3 a infant school **b** national school **c** secondary school
4 a infant school **b** secondary school **c** St Condletts College

Task 4

Before you listen to the cassette again, read the multiple choice questions below. You may be able to answer some of them immediately. Then listen and answer.

1 Tony's education took place
a in a college in the UK.
b at school in Dublin.
c at a university named after a saint.
d in Northern Ireland.

2 In Ireland, a national school was
a for all children.
b a free school.
c run by nuns.
d after primary school.

3 A big difference between education in the UK and in Ireland is
a the influence of the church.
b the amount you have to pay.
c the academic standards.
d the amount of religious education.

4 Until 1966, the Irish educational system
  - **a** was completely private.
  - **b** was organised in churches.
  - **c** provided compulsory education until the age of twelve.
  - **d** was a comprehensive system.

5 At the time Tony was educated, it was normal for parents
  - **a** to avoid paying for their children's education.
  - **b** to pay for bringing up their children.
  - **c** to attend school with their children.
  - **d** to save money for their children's education.

6 Until 1966, if parents couldn't afford to pay,
  - **a** they had to leave school at twelve.
  - **b** their children had to leave school at midday.
  - **c** the children had to leave at the age of twelve.
  - **d** they could continue in school.

7 Tony thinks that in the UK,
  - **a** education should be a right.
  - **b** there is a big difference in attitudes to education.
  - **c** there are a lot of strikes in schools.
  - **d** school pupils are very confident.

Task 5

Re-write the following extract, taking out the hesitations and other aspects of spoken English that are not necessary to convey the information.

Before that er I had been at a primary school um what in Ireland in those days was called a national school that is to say you didn't actually pay for it so I had the experience of going from a very posh infant school which was run by nuns then to this er national school where the social context was completely different from what I'd come from and then to this um rather posh secondary school.

Task 6

Now read this extract and mark the words that you expect to be stressed.

Ken And would you call it a comprehensive system, as we call it in Britain?

Tony No, absolutely not a comprehensive system. I mean, that's where it is completely different. In addition to being dominated by the church until 1966, I think, virtually all education in Ireland was private, you had to pay for it. That's why I mentioned this national school I went to. There you didn't pay but everybody only had compulsory and state-provided education to the age of twelve. That did change in '66 but the generation that I came from was very much brought up … er … on the idea that you had to pay for education and parents would save in order to provide children with a secondary school opportunity. In that respect, it's very like certain countries in Europe where parents work hard specially to provide education for their children so … no, it's not at all a comprehensive system. Not at all.

Now listen again to see if you were right.

Task 7

'People seem to think that education is a right that they can confidently expect.'

This is Tony's opinion about British attitudes to education. Do you think education is a right? Do children value their education more if they know their parents have made sacrifices to pay for it?

SPEAKING Occupations

Task 1

Look at the people in the photograph. What do they do? Make a list of the occupations that they might have. Are some easier to guess than others?

Task 2

Look at the three lists below. They are all requirements for different kinds of jobs. Check that you understand the meaning of all the words and phrases. What kind of jobs do they relate to?

skills	confident	good eyesight
experience	enthusiastic	stamina
qualifications	numerate	fitness
training	literate	strength
apprenticeship	articulate	calmness under pressure
a degree	committed	a good head for heights
exam passes	sociable	good balance

What is the difference between the words in the three columns?

Task 3

What skills, experience and/or training are required for the occupations you have allocated to the people in the photograph? Use the following expressions to express your views:

To be a (doctor), you need to study for at least seven years.

... you need to have very good examination results.

... you need to be very committed.

You have to train/learn a trade/study/be an apprentice.

Task 4

(In pairs) Ask and answer questions about the photograph using the prompts below.

a What/ you/ think/ man/ dark suit/ does?

b Why/ you/ think/ that?

c What qualifications/ you/ need/ job/ like that?

d You/ like/ do/ that job?

e What kind/ job/ you/ like/ have?

Task 5

Read the following three passages.

Which one is

1 a description of someone's own experience?
2 a description of skills probably required for a job?
3 an advertisement for a job?

a I expect you'd have to be quite tall and strong and very fit. They would probably want you to have lots of stamina and perhaps some ability with self defence or martial arts. And I suppose you would have to know something about the law.

b Perfect eyesight, great self confidence, the ability to be calm under pressure and stamina are all essential requirements. A degree or equivalent qualification in maths and/or physics are desirable. Flying experience is not necessary as full training will be given.

c I worked as a manager with the local authority for five years, not in the Housing Department but in the Social Services Department, so I was in contact with the same kind of people. And I also spent a year doing Voluntary Service Overseas, working on a housing project in Africa.

Task 6

Which of the following occupations are being referred to in the three passages above?

- housing officer
- policeman
- pilot
- doctor
- clothes designer
- farm worker

Express in your own words what each passage in Task 5 is.

Example It's a description of the skills you need to be a ...

Task 7

Now describe the skills necessary for the three occupations listed in Task 6 which were not dealt with in the reading passages.

Task 8

Role-play (in pairs)

Student A You are applying for an unusual or dangerous job.

Student B You are the interviewer. You must prepare as many difficult questions as you can think of. Work out the interview and then act it out for the rest of the class. You can choose an occupation from the list below or think of another one.

- aircraft test pilot
- motor racing driver
- politician's bodyguard
- lion tamer
- steeplejack

Task 9

Discussion Which is more important in a new job—experience or enthusiasm? Divide into two groups and discuss it, then compare your ideas with the other group.

Exam practice: paper 4 LISTENING COMPREHENSION

FIRST PART

For questions **1–6** tick (✓) one of the boxes, **A**, **B**, **C** or **D**.

1 Agatha Miller was

A an American born in England.
B the daughter of an American.
C born in America.
D an actress born in Torquay.

2 Her mother claimed to be able to

A predict the future.
B read very quickly.
C tell fortunes.
D discover what people were thinking.

3 Agatha's brother

A was a very practical person.
B wanted to be a comedian.
C played tricks on people.
D told a lot of jokes.

4 Her work during the First World War

A led to her marriage to a pilot.
B was for the air force.
C taught her about murder mysteries.
D gave her information she used when writing.

5 Agatha Miller is better known as the writer

A Julie Christie.
B Henry Miller.
C Agatha Christie.
D Arthur Miller.

6 Her books are very successful because

A they have been translated into 44 languages.
B people are enthusiastic about them.
C you keep reading them until you know who committed the crime.
D everyone agrees about her skill.

SECOND PART

For questions **7–13**, tick (✓) whether the statements are true or false.

		True	False
7	There are more insects in Brazil than in other countries.		
8	A flea can jump 30,000 times higher than a human.		
9	A flea's acceleration when jumping is faster than a moon rocket.		
10	Ticks drink the blood of other creatures.		
11	Ticks can survive starvation for 25 years.		
12	A honey bee can tell other honey bees where to find nectar.		
13	The other bees then follow the first bee back to the source of the nectar.		

THIRD PART

Fill in the missing information in the application form.

APPLICATION FORM

Full name *Michael John* ______

Address *26* ______ *Square, Reading*

A-levels *English, German and* ______

Degree in *Russian and* ______

From ______ *University*

Languages spoken *1. Russian* *2. German* *3. French* *4.* ______

Fluency *1. Fluent* *2.* ______ *3.* ______ *4. Elementary*

Business qualifications **MBA** ☐ **Yes** ☐ **No**

Word processing ☐ **Yes** ☐ **No**

FOURTH PART

Fill in the missing information.

Parke Thompson of ______ USA and Giorgio Ricatto of ______ Italy are the world's most travelled men. They have both visited all ______ of the world's sovereign states.

David Kunst, an American, walked round the world between June ______ and October ______.

Tomas Carlos Pereira from ______ spent ten years walking ______ kilometres around five continents.

John Lees from Brighton holds the record for the ______ walk across the USA.

Looking back

LISTENING 1 The early years of the 20th century

Task 1

On the cassette, you will hear an interview with a lady who can remember what life was like in the early part of the 20th century. Which of the following things do you expect her to refer to?

air travel	coal fires	the First World War
suffragettes	television	street markets
trams	cinemas	cassette recorders

Task 2

The lady being interviewed was born in 1910, the youngest child in a large family. Before you listen to the cassette, read the following statements and decide if they are possible or impossible.

a She met Queen Victoria.
b She had brothers who were soldiers in the 1914–18 war.
c She married a man who was born in the 19th century.
d Her oldest sister was born in 1890.
e Her mother was in France during the French Revolution.

Task 3

Now listen to the cassette and answer the multiple choice questions below. Quickly read the questions before listening. It will give you an idea of what to expect.

1 Nellie Williamson was born
a just before her father died.
b during the First World War.
c after two brothers had been killed.
d just after her father died.

2 Her father worked
a as a writer.
b for a solicitor.
c as a solicitor.
d for a marvellous company.

3 When she was a child, the family lived
a in a small house in Rochester.
b in a hotel.
c in a house with three rooms.
d in Lancashire.

4 She attended a church school where she had to
a wear a hat at all times.
b fight with her sisters.
c get up early.
d attend church on Friday mornings.

5 When she left school, her first job was
a in the ticket office of a theatre.
b as a clerk for the transport department.
c shovelling coal.
d working in a cellar.

6 She met her husband
a on holiday.
b at work.
c at a dance.
d at church.

Task 4

Below is a list of words and expressions that Nellie uses. Look at the three possible definitions, listen to the cassette again and decide which is the most likely.

1 *in service*
a working
b being used
c working as a servant

2 *scullery*
a a bedroom
b a garden
c a room near the kitchen

3 *grid*
a a bar on the window
b a cover over a hole in the ground
c an electrical installation

4 *shovel*
a a spade
b a brush
c a cloth

Task 5

In the extract below, some of the words have been changed. Listen again and mark the words that are wrong.

Nellie I went to St Ambrose school, chair school, where we had to go to church every Friday mourning. We weren't aloud in church without a cat and so there was always a fire between my sisters and myself to find a cat.

Ken Tell me something about the way, for example, that houses were eaten. What did you do for eating?

Nellie With a cold fire. We used to have the cold delivered in the stream and we had grids in the street where the cold went down into the seller and it was our John when we came home from school to shuffle all this cold into the seller.

Task 6

What are the main differences between urban life today and when Nellie was a young woman? Make a list of the most obvious ones.

LISTENING 2 The History Quiz

Task 1

The History Quiz is a radio quiz where all the questions are about historical events and famous people from the past. Below are some of the people who are mentioned in the quiz. Write down anything you know about them.

John Kennedy	Napoleon Bonaparte	Karl Marx
Giuseppe Garibaldi	George Washington	Mao Tse-Tung
Mahatma Gandhi	Neil Armstrong	Buzz Aldrin

Discuss them with other students and add to what you have written.

Task 2

The radio quiz is about historical events. Which of the following words do you expect to hear?

caused	ended	became	painted	was born
assassinated	sang	set foot on	played	took place
cooked	led	listened	began	recognised

Task 3

On the right is a list of the names of the contestants in the History Quiz. When you listen to the cassette for the first time, simply write down the number of points that the three gained after the first fifteen questions. (One point for each correct answer).

Contestants	Number of points
Shirley Grant	
Michael Rimmer	
Christine Burrows	

Task 4

Listen to the cassette again and this time concentrate on the *answers* to the fifteen questions. If you can, write them in the chart . Some of the answers have been filled in to help you.

1 George Washington	**9**
2	**10** Trier, Germany
3	**11**
4 Dallas, Texas	**12** The attack on Pearl Harbor
5	**13**
6	**14**
7	**15**
8 He wanted to unify Italy	

Task 5

In the second part of the History Quiz, there are seven questions to be answered by the radio listeners. The answers are printed below, but they are printed in the wrong order. Read the answers and try to imagine what the questions might be.

	Question number
a He wrote *War and Peace.*	
b She was the wife of Louis XIV of France.	
c Because he wanted to marry a divorced woman.	
d She was the only double Nobel Prize Winner.	
e Simon Bolivar.	
f He was the first person to climb Mount Everest.	1
g He invented the telephone.	

Task 6

Now listen to the second part of the History Quiz and read the answers at the same time. Put the number of the question in the box beside the relevant answer. The first one has been done for you.

Task 7

/ɜː/ or /aɪ/ or /ɪ/?

The names of the three contestants in the History Quiz are Shirley /ʃɜːlɪ/, Michael /Maɪkəl/ and Christine /Krɪstiːn/. All the words below are from the cassette and they all contain one of the key vowel sounds. Put them in the appropriate column: *Shirley* /ɜː/, *Michael* /aɪ/, *Christine* /ɪ/.

first	fingers	Chinese	fifteen	five
listeners	quiz	earth	history	thirty
India	designed	think	Italy	United

Task 8

In groups, write a History Quiz, in English, about your country. Ask your questions to other groups.

SPEAKING Old houses

Task 1

Look at the photograph. How many different parts of the building can you name? Use your dictionary to look up any words that you don't know.

Task 2

Below are descriptions of three houses, which are taken from three different novels. There may be some words and phrases that you don't understand. Read each extract silently first and then read it aloud to another student. Then listen to the other student reading it back to you. Don't look at the words while you are listening.

a The house was low, was once white with a deep front porch and green shutters but had long ago darkened to the color of the slate-grey yard around it. Rain-rotten shingles drooped over the eaves of the veranda. (*To Kill a Mockingbird*, by Harper Lee)

b The house was a rather gloomy double-fronted facade in a small street near Berkeley Square: the pillars of the entrance flanked on either side with hollow cones for the linkmen to extinguish their torches. (*A Question of Upbringing*, by Anthony Powell)

c The place was full of dust and spiderwebs, and looked thoroughly abandoned ... the entire house was carpeted with a thick layer of grass, dust and dried-out leaves. It smelled like a tomb. Estaban heard the faint passage of the rats in the rafters. (*The House of the Spirits*, by Isabel Allende)

Task 3

The houses described above are in the following locations:

- London, England
- the Southern USA
- Latin America

Can you match the locations and the descriptions? Are there any clues which help you?

Task 4

Look up any words that you don't know and discuss the following questions with another student.

a Two of the houses appear to be neglected. Which two?

b Which word in the second description suggests that there is very little light?

c What do you think 'rain-rotten' means?

d You can sit outside at the front of one of these houses. Which one? How do you know?

e Which description gives you the best idea of the colour of the house?

Exam practice: paper 5 INTERVIEW

PERSON A

SECTION 1

1

2

3

a The jet engine was actually invented in 1907 but these turbo propeller planes are still flying commercially in the 1990s.

b The last steam engines were seen in Britain in the early seventies, although they survived much longer in other countries.

c They were big, powerful vehicles, but they were designed for elegance rather than speed. They had little aerodynamic styling and they used a lot of petrol.

SECTION 2

1 a 'Style has disappeared. Everything you see is functional, not beautiful.'

b 'Transport is safer, quieter and cleaner than it has ever been before.'

2

1988 BMW CONVERTIBLE Stereo, carphone, very fast. Only £5,000	**1937 BENTLEY** Needs a lot of attention, but a beautiful car. Very rare. £10,000
1963 VOLVO 30 years old but in perfect condition. £750	**1991 NISSAN SUNNY** Excellent car, stereo, sun-roof, alarm system. Very good value, £3,995

3
- a motor-bike
- an air-conditioned bus
- a Land Rover
- a helicopter
- a train with a sleeper compartment

Exam practice: paper 5 INTERVIEW

PERSON B

SECTION 1

Photographs Ask your partner to study the three photographs in Section 1. Open a discussion using these suggestions:

Describe/compare
- the age of the plane, car and train
- their style

Discuss
- the difference in modern design
- the qualities of the older designs
- what styles have disappeared

If you are working with a group, encourage an individual to start a discussion. Invite other students to answer.

Passages Ask your partner or the group to read the three passages and to link the themes of the passages and the photographs. Invite comments on where the extracts may have been taken from.

SECTION 2

Now choose one of the following activities:

1 **Discussion** Invite your partner or the group to discuss one or both of the following topics. Use the suggested prompts, if necessary.

a 'Style has disappeared. Everything you see is functional, not beautiful.'

Prompts
- Designers used to pay more attention to the look of a car.
- Trains and planes are no longer designed to look beautiful inside.
- There is too much plastic in modern design.

b 'Transport is safer, quieter and cleaner than it has ever been before.'

Prompts
- Cars, planes and trains all use cleaner and more efficient fuel.
- The noise from all forms of transport has been reduced.
- Safety is now the most important design feature.

2 **Activity 1** Tell your partner or the group to look at the advertisements for second-hand cars. Ask them to choose the one they would buy and to give reasons.

1988 BMW CONVERTIBLE Stereo, carphone, very fast. Only £5,000	**1937 BENTLEY** Needs a lot of attention, but a beautiful car. Very rare. £10,000
1963 VOLVO 30 years old but in perfect condition. £750	**1991 NISSAN SUNNY** Excellent car, stereo, sun-roof, alarm system. Very good value, £3,995

3 **Activity 2** Ask your partner or the group to study the list of means of transport. Ask which one they would prefer to use for a long journey (eg more than 1,000 kilometres).
- a motor-bike
- an air-conditioned bus
- a Land Rover
- a helicopter
- a train with a sleeper compartment

Free time

LISTENING 1 What do you do in your spare time?

Task 1

In her spare time, Helen Wood is a Samaritan. The Samaritans is an organisation which helps lonely, depressed and suicidal people. It is part of an international organisation called Befrienders International.

Before you listen to the cassette, make sure you know the meanings of the followings words and expressions.

pressure	shocked	level-headed
widowed	stressful	voluntary work
horrified	compassionate	overnight shift

Task 2

Now listen to the cassette. Make a note of the following information:

- What kind of people call the Samaritans?
- How much time does Helen spend there?
- How many branches of the Samaritans are there worldwide?

Task 3

Choose the more suitable meaning for the following expressions from the conversation.

1 *people who can't match up to the pressures*
  a people who can't make a connection between the pressures
  b people who can't manage the pressures

2 *someone objective*
  a someone independent
  b someone you don't like

3 *completely confidential*
  a not nervous at all
  b no one else will know

4 *you'll have their full attention*
  a they will wait for you
  b they will concentrate on your problem

5 *the phones are manned*
  a there's someone by the phone
  b there's someone on the phone

Task 4

Below is the text of Helen's answer to the first question she is asked. But some of the words have been omitted from the written version. Listen again and indicate (ʎ) when you hear something which is not written.

I think we live in a society that moves very quickly and doesn't find time for people who can't match up to the pressures that are put on them. It's for people who are without support at a stressful time and it's often there for people who have support and friends they could talk to but it's something very private that they'd rather take elsewhere to someone objective. So the service offers something which is always there … it's befriending without questioning, it's completely confidential, you'll find a warm response, someone there to listen to whatever you say, whatever the problem is. They won't be shocked or bored, you'll have their full attention and care and I think it's something that we don't always find.

Task 5

Look at the list of hobbies and spare time activities below. Are any of them unusual, strange, or dangerous? Do you do any of these things?

Collecting: stamps old pencils butterflies clocks autographs

Walking: in the mountains on the beach along railway lines in the countryside on walls

Painting pictures of: bus stops animals litter trees old people

Singing: in the bath on the roof in a choir in a rock band on the bus

Task 6

What do *you* do in your spare time? Talk to other students and see which hobbies you share.

LISTENING 2 The Millbrook Arts Festival

Task 1

On the cassette, there is an interview with a man who is organising an arts festival for the first time. Make a list of the events you might expect to find in the programme of an arts festival.

Task 2

The organiser is hoping to hold the arts festival in a small village, and this presents him with a number of problems. Look at the list below of possible problems he faces. Which three do you think are the most important?

- accommodation and parking facilities
- vandalism
- persuading artistes and performers to attend
- choosing the date
- finding auditoria and theatre space
- selling enough tickets
- advertising the event

Task 3

Below are five extracts from the interview. They all contain a different *phrasal verb*. Decide which of the possible meanings is correct.

1 *The villagers were a bit* ***put out****.*
  a They had to leave their houses. **b** They were upset.

2 *Everyone can see what's* ***going on****.*
  a Everyone can see what's happening. **b** Everyone can see what will happen.

3 *I haven't* ***worked*** *that* ***out*** *yet.*
  a I haven't finished that yet. **b** I haven't solved that problem yet.

4 *Will the villagers* ***put*** *the visitors* ***up****?*
  a Will the villagers annoy the visitors? **b** Will they accommodate the visitors?

5 *We'll* ***carry on*** *living our lives.*
  a We'll continue living our lives. **b** We'll complain about our lives.

Task 4

Now listen to the cassette. Listen specifically for the following words and expressions. Try to work out the meaning from the context.

a golden opportunity   a stage   television celebrities   a sponsor
a slope   cabaret acts   a marquee

Task 5

Look at the multiple choice questions below. Read them quickly to get an idea of what you have to answer. Now listen to the cassette again and choose the correct answer.

1 Millbrook is a village where a conference centre
  a recently opened.
  b staged an arts festival.
  c opened two years ago.
  d is being planned.

2 The opening of the conference centre caused
  a more traffic to use the village.
  b some of the villagers to leave.
  c a great deal of interest.
  d Mr Field to take action.

3 Mr Field intends to build a stage
  a at the top of the slope.
  b in the middle of the lake.
  c in the garden of the conference centre.
  d in a marquee.

4 A number of television personalities
  a will attend the arts festival.
  b are certain to attend.
  c are organising the arts festival.
  d have been invited to come.

5 A marquee will be erected
  a because it never rains in Millbrook.
  b to persuade the Royal Shakespeare Company to come.
  c so that the festival can continue in the rain.
  d in order to cover the stage.

6 Mr Field needs to find a sponsor
  a because he hasn't got much money.
  b in case he doesn't sell many tickets.
  c to help him work out the cost.
  d because it's a big commercial operation.

7 Because of a lack of tourist accommodation,
  a visitors will be unable to stay.
  b the villagers will have to put up with it.
  c the church will arrange everything.
  d Mr Field hopes the villagers will help.

Task 6

Read the introduction to the interview (below) and mark the words that you would expect to be *unstressed* in spoken English.

And now some local news. The village of Millbrook, which is about thirty miles south of Bristol, is not somewhere that you immediately associate with the arts. There are no cinemas or theatres there, and no auditorium where you could put on a concert. But there is a big new conference centre and one local resident has decided that he would like to organise an arts festival there. Sarah Thompson went to see how he was getting on.

Now listen to the introduction again on the cassette. What kind of words are generally unstressed?

Task 7

The words 'local' /ləʊkəl/ and 'south' /saʊθ/ appear in the extract above. Now read the extract below, and mark any words that include the sounds /əʊ/ and /aʊ/.

Millbrook has three thousand inhabitants, two churches, three pubs, a restaurant and a large conference centre, which opened about two years ago. Some of the villagers were a bit put out by the conference centre, which has led to a big increase in traffic through the village. One particular resident, however, has decided that the conference centre presents the village with a golden opportunity. The resident is Mr Rupert Field. Mr Field, what gave you the idea of holding an arts festival at the conference centre?

Now listen again to see if you were right.

Task 8

Mr Field makes no reference to any activities at his arts festival designed for young people or children. What do you think he should include for younger visitors?

Task 9

Why do you think the village is called *Millbrook*?

SPEAKING Winners and losers

Task 1

Look at the two photographs on this page. Describe them. Ask other students these questions:

a Who/ people/ photographs? They/ famous?
b You/ know/ names? You/ know/ where/ they/ from?
c What kind/ events/ attending?
d When/ where/ these events/ take place?
e What/ main difference/ two events/ people/ attend?
f What/ people/ photographs/ just/ won?

If you're not sure, you can express your uncertainty like this:

I'm not (absolutely) sure, but I think s/he's ...
I don't know for certain, but I think ...
I may be wrong, but isn't s/he ... ?
If I remember rightly, s/he's ...
Am I right in thinking that s/he's ...

And if you want to express your uncertainty about *when* the events took place, here are few useful expressions:

a couple of years ago
three or four years ago
(some time) in the last three or four years
not too long ago
not that long ago

1

2

Task 2

Read the three passages below. They are all connected with sport, but they are all from different sources. Are they spoken or written? Are they from an interview? From a book? What kind of book?

a This is the proudest moment of my life. A gold medal and a world record. It's a victory for the whole team and for the country, not just for me. And I couldn't have done it without the support of my family and friends.

b The match between Miss Capriati and Miss Sanchez will now take place on Court Number Two, not Court Number One. The Junior Championship Final, which was to have taken place on Court Number Two, will now take place on Court Number Twelve. We apologise for these changes and the delays, which have been caused by the unexpected downpour.

c Of course no one knew about the drugs he was using at the time and no one was more shocked than I was when the story broke. I heard about it as I was leaving the training ground and I immediately went to find Ben to sympathise with him, but he had already left for the airport. I think that was when I decided to write this book.

Task 3

Choose the possible sources of the passages from this list.

1 a news item about a tennis match
2 a sporting autobiography
3 words spoken by a proud parent
4 a newspaper article about the use of drugs
5 a speech by an Olympic winner
6 an announcement at a tennis tournament

Task 4

Discuss your choice of the sources with another student. Which words or phrases made you decide that the source was possible or unlikely?

Task 5

Role-play You have planned an artistic event in your town and you want to invite a famous person (eg a local politician) to attend.

Act out the telephone conversation with the person you want to invite. This will be a formal conversation and here are some expressions that you might find useful:

I'm sure you're extremely busy but …

We'd (very much) like you to attend …

Is there any chance that you might …?

Everybody would be (absolutely) delighted if you would …

You should tell the person what will be going on at the artistic event and what you would like her or him to do. Make a speech? Give prizes?

Task 6

Discussion Politics and sport. In the last twenty years, there have been a series of boycotts of major sporting events such as the Olympic Games for political reasons.

Do you think politics and sport should be separate or are they always going to be mixed? Discuss this in groups, make notes and report back to the whole class.

Exam practice: paper 4 LISTENING COMPREHENSION

FIRST PART

Fill in the missing names.

	Last week's team	Next week's team
Goalkeeper	O'Toole	O'Toole
Defence	Hunt Smith Bagley Racket	Hunt ______ Bradley ______
Midfield	Cross Purvis	Cross ______
Attack	Barton Matthews Henry Higgins	______ ______ Matthews Henry
Substitutes	Burton Rowe	Barton ______

SECOND PART

Fill in the missing days and times below.

Appointment with Mr Shilton on Thursday at _____.

Choir practice on _____ at _____.

Exhibition of Welsh artists on _____ evening.

Dinner with Angela on _____.

Game of squash with Paul on _____ at _____.

Parents' visit on _____ _____.

Lunch with Jonathan on _____.

THIRD PART

Fill in next year's expenditure.

GARTON CITY COUNCIL BUDGET		
Item	Current year	Next year
Education	12 million	
Social Services	4 million	
Lighting, cleaning	million	
Leisure and recreation	3 million	
Housing	6 million	
Police	3 million	
Ethnic minorities	million	
Administration	5 million	
TOTALS	**34 MILLION**	**31 MILLION**

FOURTH PART

For questions **1–7** tick (✓) one of the boxes **A**, **B**, **C**, or **D**).

1 Alan Dibble is

A a Scottish radio presenter.	**A**
B a fund-raising cyclist.	**B**
C a round-the-world pilot.	**C**
D a hospital worker.	**D**

2 After riding from Edinburgh to London, he intends to

A find some TV cameras.	**A**
B visit the Houses of Parliament.	**B**
C talk on radio and TV.	**C**
D meet the Prime Minister.	**D**

3 When he reaches the Continent, he will

A take the Hovercraft.	**A**
B fly to Athens.	**B**
C take the pretty route to Athens.	**C**
D cycle to Greece.	**D**

4 Two years ago, he cycled

A 5,000 kilometres around Scotland.	**A**
B where there are a lot of Scots.	**B**
C across a North American country.	**C**
D round the east of Canada.	**D**

5 The radio interviewer mistakenly believes that

A Karachi is in India.	**A**
B Dubai is near Pakistan.	**B**
C Karachi is in Pakistan.	**C**
D Dubai is in India.	**D**

6 He hopes to arrive in Australia

A at a place with a Scottish name.	**A**
B directly from Karachi.	**B**
C with his friends.	**C**
D on a boat from Perth.	**D**

7 Alan is going to cycle to Sydney

A and then fly to Britain.	**A**
B after staying with friends.	**B**
C the easy way.	**C**
D from Los Angeles.	**D**

Getting away from it all

LISTENING 1 Air travel

Task 1

When you go to an airport to catch a plane, you have to do the things which are listed below. Put them in the correct order. If you've never flown, you can guess the correct order, or get help from someone who has been on an aeroplane.

a get a boarding card
b wait in the departure lounge
c go to the airport
d listen to the safety instructions
e check in
f get on the plane
g go through passport control (if it's an international flight)
h take off

Task 2

There are safety instructions in a leaflet that you can usually find in the seat pocket in front of you on the plane. See page 59 for an example. On the cassette, you'll hear a member of the cabin staff explaining the instructions. Which of the following things do you expect her to refer to?

What to do if

- the No Smoking sign is switched on
- you feel sick
- there is a reduction in air pressure
- the plane is about to take off
- you don't like the food
- there is an emergency
- you can't fasten your seat-belt
- you're on the wrong plane

Task 3

Which of the following words and phrases would you expect to hear in a safety instruction announcement?

high-heeled shoes	driver	unlikely	seat pocket
life-jacket	straps	aisles	discussion
emergency	permitted	entertainment	underneath

Task 4

Now listen to the cassette and tick (✓) the words from the list above that you hear.

Task 5

Below is a check-list of the safety instructions that you heard on the cassette. They are not written in the order that you heard them. Try to put them in the correct order without listening to the cassette again. The first one has been indicated to help you.

a life-jackets	
b preparation for take-off	
c emergency exits	1
d no-smoking areas	
e seat-belts	
f oxygen masks	

Now listen to the cassette again to see if you were right.

Task 6

The following verbs were used in the announcement:

remove *inflate* *extinguish*

Each of these verbs could be replaced by one of the following *phrasal verbs.* Which ones?

take in	take off	take to
blow out	blow down	blow up
put up	put on	put out

Task 7

Read the following extract from the safety announcement and underline the words which you think should be stressed in spoken English.

For your information and safety, please read the instruction booklet in the seat pocket in front of you. Now, in preparation for take-off, please make sure that your seat-belt is securely fastened, your seat is in the upright position and the table in front of you is folded away.

Now listen to the cassette again and compare.

LISTENING 2 Holiday phone-in

Task 1

You're going to hear an extract from a radio programme where listeners phone in to give advice to other listeners about holidays—where to go and what to do when you get there. Below are three expressions that you will hear. Before you listen to the cassette, choose the correct definition for each expression.

1 *package deal*
- **a** the cost of sending a parcel by post
- **b** a business arrangement about packaging
- **c** a way of organising travel and accommodation at the same time

2 *holiday brochures*
- **a** tourist guides
- **b** information booklets
- **c** hotel accommodation

3 *advance booking*
- **a** reading difficult books
- **b** reserving before you go
- **c** money given to writers

Task 2

Below are the names of *six* people who telephoned the programme. You are only going to hear three of them. Read the list quickly before you listen to the cassette. On the right is a list of the holidays that they talked about. As you listen, tick (✓) the three people that you hear, and the holidays that they talk about.

1 Gill from South London
2 Anna from North Wales
3 Hazel from Brighton
4 Graham from Leeds
5 David from Edinburgh
6 Tim from Bournemouth

a islands in the Indian Ocean
b going on safari in Kenya
c a cruise in the Caribbean
d Spanish paradors
e across the States by train
f driving across the USA

Task 3

Now listen to the cassette again. This time, concentrate on the *advice* given by each caller. Look at the sentences below and choose the most appropriate ending for each one.

1 The first caller advised listeners
- **a** to avoid travelling from Paris.
- **b** not to book a hotel before leaving.
- **c** to ignore the mosquitoes.

2 The second caller suggested
- **a** exploring the Spanish coastline.
- **b** flying to the capital of Spain.
- **c** staying in modern hotels.

3 The third caller's advice was
- **a** to book a return flight to New York.
- **b** to drive across America.
- **c** not to drive dangerously.

Task 4

Look at the following extract from the radio programe. Look particularly at the questions asked by Gerry Sutton. Before listening to the cassette again,decide whether the intonation rises (↗) or falls (↘) at the end of each question.

Gerry What are you going to tell us about, Tim?

Tim Paradors.

Gerry What?

Tim Paradors.

Gerry What are paradors?

Tim Accommodation for tourists in Spain.

Gerry You mean hotels?

Tim No, they're not hotels.

Gerry What are they, then?

Now listen to the cassette again and check the intonation.

Task 5

/θ/ or /ð/?

All the following words appear on the cassette. Is the 'th' voiced or voiceless?

the	thanks	nothing	those
thought	that	there	north
they	south	them	Bournemouth

SPEAKING Instructions and advice

Task 1

Look at the extract from an airline safety instruction card below. Think about how to express what the illustrations mean in simple instructions.

a

b

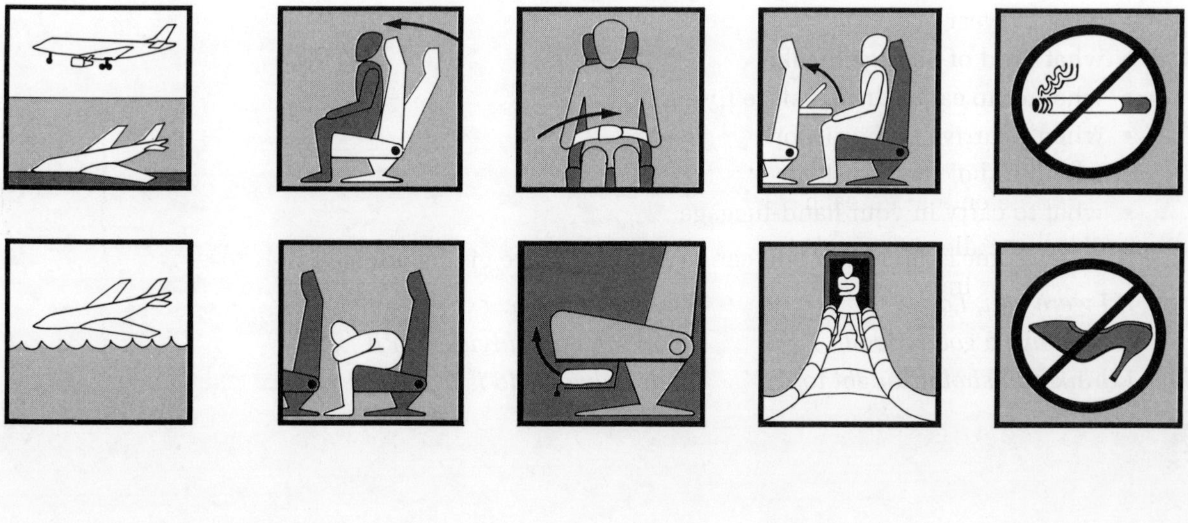

Task 2

Write down four instructions for **a** and four instructions for **b**. Are some of them more difficult to express than others? Use your dictionary if necessary, and listen to the airline safety announcement on the cassette. Here are some new words that may be useful:

straighten *brace* *chute* *landing*

Task 3

Think about what you could say if you were asked about the illustrations and what they mean. Make notes about the following:

a Why do you think the instruction card has illustrations?

b Why are there no words?

c Why are there no photographs?

d As there is usually a safety demonstration before the plane takes off, why do you think there is a safety instruction booklet at all?

Task 4

Look at the following pieces of advice about flying. Do you think it is good advice or bad advice? Make notes about your thoughts, even if you have never flown in an aeroplane.

a Always keep your seat-belt fastened, even when the Fasten Seat-belt sign is switched off.

b Listen to your own cassettes on your own walkman ... otherwise you'll get bored.

c Get a non-smoking seat even if you intend to smoke. You can always go to the smoking section if you want a cigarette.

d Don't get a seat on the aisle. You have to keep getting up to let people get past.

Role-play Giving advice. Act out a conversation between someone who has never flown in an aeroplane and a regular flier.

The first-time flier could ask questions about the following:

- what to wear
- what kind of luggage to take
- whether to eat or drink before flying
- when to arrive at the airport
- what kind of seat to ask for
- what to carry in your hand-luggage

Here are some expressions you can use when you're giving advice:

If I were you, I'd ...	*Why don't you ...?*
It's always a good idea to ...	*If you take my advice, you'll ...*
I think you should/ought to ...	*What I always do is this ...*

Exam practice: paper 5 INTERVIEW

PERSON A

SECTION 1

1

2

3

a With the depletion of the ozone layer, the sun's rays are more harmful than ever. If you intend to lie on the beach this summer, make sure you take plenty of sun-blocking creams.

b Acquasun Holidays are highly recommended, but a word of warning: you should really be a very good swimmer if you want to try all their activities.

c Experienced guides accompany all parties, so there is no danger. Of course, it helps if you've done some climbing before, but beginners are welcome at Lyndale Lodge.

SECTION 2

1
- a family with seven children
- a husband and wife in their 80s
- a woman travelling alone
- twelve workers from the same factory

2 'Well, one of us is wrong.'

3 **Role A** You are a fitness fanatic.
Role B You love tennis and swimming.
Role C You like classical music concerts and theatre performances.

PERSON B

SECTION 1

Photographs Ask your partner to study the three photographs. Open a discussion using these suggestions:

Describe/compare

- the locations
- the weather conditions
- the people

Discuss

- why people choose a particular holiday
- why people choose dangerous hobbies
- the value of holidays

If you are working with a group, encourage an individual to start a discussion. Invite other students to answer.

Passages Ask your partner or the group to read the three passages and to link the themes of the passages and the photographs. Invite comments on where the extracts may have been taken from.

SECTION 2

Now choose one of the following activities:

1 **Discussion** Ask your partner or the group to consider which holiday would be most suitable for the following people:

- a family with seven children
- a husband and wife in their 80s
- a woman travelling alone
- twelve workers from the same factory

2 **Activity** Tell your partner or the group to look at the cartoon and ask these questions:

a Where are the people standing?
b What kind of holiday are they preparing for?
c What do you think the explanation is?

3 **Discussion (for pairs or groups)** Tell the group that they are at a meeting where the local authority is discussing how to attract more tourists to their area. They should give ideas about the facilities that the town should offer. The students should choose a role from this list.

Role A You are a fitness fanatic.
Role B You love tennis and swimming.
Role C You like classical music concerts and theatre performances.

9 Expressing obligation, necessity, permission and prohibition

Keeping fit and eating right

LISTENING 1 Playing for the Ealing Eagles

Task 1

The Ealing Eagles are an American Football team based in West London. Adam and Toby Leaver, two eighteen-year-old twins, both play for the Eagles. Before you listen to the cassette, write down anything that you know about American Football.

Task 2

Which of the following words would you expect to hear in a conversation about a team sport like American football?

silent	attack	boring	practise
rules	singing	defence	market
training	dangerous	unlucky	personal

Task 3

Read the True or False exercise below. Then listen to the cassette and tick (✓) the appropriate box.

	True	False
a American Football is still an unusual sport in the United Kingdom.		
b Both the twins were interested in sport at school.		
c They first played American Football when they were living in New York.		
d It wasn't easy to get into a team in England.		
e In an American Football game, players are not always on the field.		
f During training, the twins have to pull cars round a field.		
g They think the game is dangerous because of the protective clothing they have to wear.		
h Their father would have liked to play the game.		

Task 4

/ɪ/ or /iː/?

In the extract below, a number of words have been omitted. Each omitted word contains *either* the sound /ɪ/, as in the word 'fit' *or* the sound /iː/, as in the word 'feet'. Listen and write **1** if the sound is /ɪ/ and **2** if the sound is /iː/. (You don't need to write in the word itself.) The first letter of the omitted words is there to help you.

Toby There aren't any t_(2)_ near where we l_____. We had to travel about twenty miles to find one. And it wasn't e_____ to get into the team. They make sure that you're really i_____ before they let you come along to practise. And then you have to wait w_____ before they decide i_____ they want you to join.

Adam That's right, but I t_____ they were p_(1)_ p_(2)_ to s_____ us because we're both quite b_____ and strong, but we also know the rules. They have a lot of difficulty w_____ some of the new players because the rules can be a b_____ complicated.

Task 5

Are any of the following sports dangerous? Make a list of the ones you think are dangerous and give your reasons.

motor-racing	soccer	golf	skiing
mountaineering	tennis	fencing	parachuting
marathon running	basketball	hang-gliding	weight-lifting

LISTENING 2 Foods that fight

Task 1

This section is a discussion about the food that you should eat if you want to feel better or lose weight. Below is a list of words and expressions that you need to know before you listen to the cassette. Look them up in your dictionary, if necessary.

overweight	fattening	fast food
helpings (of food)	seconds (of food)	carbohydrate
protein	source	lose your temper

Task 2

Read the list of words and expressions below, which also appear on the cassette. Divide them into groups of three words and expressions which have more or less the same meaning.

cut down on	rubbish	reduce the amount of	eat less	taken
eaten	nonsense	consumed	ridiculous	

Task 3

Listen to the cassette and make a note of the following:

a the names of the three people who speak

b whether they agree or disagree with each other

Task 4

Choose one sentence from the list below which reflects what each person believes:

a You shouldn't eat foods that fight.

b To lose weight, you must consume less.

c It's necessary to avoid eating meat.

d You mustn't eat potatoes and pasta.

e You should avoid fast food and fried food.

Task 5

Quickly read the multiple choice exercise below. Then listen to the cassette again and choose the correct answers.

1 The three people first speak in the following order:
- **a** Alan, Linda, Brenda
- **b** Brenda, Linda, Alan
- **c** Linda, Alan, Brenda
- **d** Brenda, Alan, Linda

2 Alan believes that if people want to lose weight,
- **a** they should miss out meals.
- **b** they've got to eat well.
- **c** eating less is the only answer.
- **d** they've got to weigh less.

3 Brenda's main argument is that
- **a** it's necessary to eat less.
- **b** you should eat good food.
- **c** people must balance good food and fast food.
- **d** Alan should eat less.

4 Brenda recommends a diet in which you
- **a** cut down on fried food and fresh vegetables.
- **b** reduce the amount of fast food that you eat.
- **c** eat less salad and fresh vegetables.
- **d** avoid fast food and cut down on fried food.

5 Linda suggests a diet which
- **a** Brenda has never heard of.
- **b** Alan agrees with.
- **c** involves eating foods that fight.
- **d** is complete nonsense.

6 The Hay Diet theory involves
- **a** eating proteins and carbohydrates on different days.
- **b** consuming different carbohydrates on different days.
- **c** avoiding meat and cheese.
- **d** eating fattening foods at the same time.

7 Alan's reaction to the Hay Diet is one of
- **a** surprise.
- **b** interest.
- **c** scorn.
- **d** disappointment.

8 Linda tells Alan that if he followed the Hay diet, he would
- **a** lose his temper very quickly.
- **b** be less aggressive.
- **c** lose weight.
- **d** eat bread and cheese every day.

Task 6

Below is the first part of the conversation. But *ten* words are wrong—they are misspelt, or they are different words which are pronounced in the same or a similar way as the correct word. Listen to the cassette and mark the words which are wrong.

Brenda So what's your advise to people who want to dye it?

Alan I think that the most important thing to tell people who won't to lose wait is this: you've got to eat less. There is simply no other weigh.

Brenda I don't agree.

Alan Listen, Brenda … most people who are overweight heat too much. The sensible thing to tell them is that they've got to cat down on what they eat.

Brenda No, I'm sorry, Alan, you're quiet wrong. People should eat a balanced diet of good food.

Alan Yes?

Brenda It isn't necessary to eat last. It's simply necessary to eat will.

Task 1

Look at the photograph above. In pairs, ask and answer the questions below. Use your dictionary if you need to.

a How old/ you/ think/ boys?
b Where/ you/ think/ they/ from?
c Can/ you/ describe/ equipment?
d What kind/ training/ you/ think/ they/ receive?

Task 2

In groups, discuss the training that the boys receive. Make a list of three things they *must do*, and three things they're *not allowed to do*.

Task 3

Read and discuss these questions. Look at the notes in Task 4 to help you answer them.

a Is either community or military service compulsory in your country? (If the answer is 'yes', answer questions **b** to **e**. If the answer is 'no', go directly to questions **f** and **g**.)
b Do boys *and* girls have to do community or military service in your country?
c How long does it last?
d How old are you when you have to do it?
e Can you do it in your home town or do you have to travel to another town?
f What do you think about compulsory community or military service?
g Do you think that boys and girls should both have to do it?

Task 4

Now read these notes:

a Questions **a** to **e** above are asking you about what happens in your country. If you know the details, you can make statements like this:
In my country, military service is compulsory for boys and girls. Boys have to do eighteen months and girls have to do one year.

b It is not a problem if you don't know or aren't sure. Look at page 52 (Unit Seven) for some useful expressions.

c Questions **f** and **g** are asking you for your *opinions.* Look at page 24 (Unit Three) for some useful expressions. Here are some ideas that may help you to express your opinion about military service:

- it helps to keep you fit
- it teaches you discipline
- you can learn a lot of new skills
- you meet a lot of people
- you can travel to different places
- it eases unemployment
- every country needs an army
- it's a waste of time
- you aren't allowed to ask the reasons for doing things
- you could be studying something useful

Task 5

Read the three passages below. Discuss them with other students. Each one indicates obligation, permission or prohibition. Which is which?

a Boys may wear their cadet uniforms at school on Fridays or on visits organised by the school, if they wish.

b Under no circumstances may cadets wear their uniforms at the weekends or during the holidays.

c Boys who wish to become cadets may only do so after receiving permission from their parents.

Which expressions tell you that the passage indicates obligation, permission or prohibition?

Task 6

Discussion (in pairs or groups) Make a list of rules you have (or had) to follow at school. Compare your list with other groups. Discuss why these rules exist and what their aims are.

Exam practice: paper 4 LISTENING COMPREHENSION

FIRST PART

Fill in the school visit chart.

	Visit one	Visit two	Visit three	Visit four
Country	Italy		USA	
When?		Easter		May
Cost	£240		£210	
Deposit by		Oct 31st		End of February
Number of places		60		

SECOND PART

Fill in the missing prices.

From Edinburgh Departing	**New York or Miami Returning**		
	By June 28th	June 29th–July 10th	July11th–August 16th
By June 14th			289
June 15th–June 27th	___		
June 28th–August 2nd	___	___	399

From Edinburgh Departing	**Los Angeles or Vancouver Returning**		
	By June 28th	June 29th–July 10th	July11th–August 16th
By June 14th			339
June 15th–June 27th	___	369	
June 28th–August 2nd	___	___	469

THIRD PART

For questions **1–5** tick (✓) one of the boxes, **A**, **B**, **C** or **D**.

1 According to Norah, actors

A have to study at drama school.	**A**
B never study at drama school.	**B**
C don't have to study at drama school.	**C**
D have simple answers	**D**

2 At Norah's drama school, all the students

A had to dress up as factory workers.	**A**
B acted like different people.	**B**
C dressed like people with different occupations.	**C**
D found it difficult to make friends.	**D**

3 After leaving acting school, Norah

A found it difficult to get an Equity card immediately.	**A**
B found it easy to get an acting job.	**B**
C wanted a job as a cabaret singer.	**C**
D joined the actors' union.	**D**

4 The Equity card system prevents

A theatre directors from working.	**A**
B people from giving jobs to their friends.	**B**
C actors from getting any work.	**C**
D cabaret singers from working as actors.	**D**

5 Norah thinks that acting is worth the effort despite

A having to work in theatres.	**A**
B being very dedicated.	**B**
C having to make a career of it.	**C**
D having hardly any money.	**D**

FOURTH PART

For questions **6–14** tick (✓) whether the statements are true or false.

		True	False
6	The idea of using guide dogs for the blind began in the 1920s.		
7	It started in Switzerland.		
8	Mrs Eustis was training dogs for the army and the police.		
9	Morris Frank was the first Swiss person to use a guide dog.		
10	Guide dogs need training which lasts for more than a year.		
11	They must learn to judge how wide a space is.		
12	Blind people must also attend the training centre before they can use a guide dog.		
13	They must spend a month there.		
14	You should take a blind person's arm when helping them across the street.		

10 Reporting events and speech; expressing opinions

Relationships

LISTENING 1 Getting married

Task 1

Which of the following words do you expect to hear in a description of a marriage ceremony?

confetti	bridegroom	disaster	reception
honeymoon	best man	service	impulsive
arranged	go-between	trial	research
property	bridesmaid	money	promise

Task 2

The first person that you will hear talking about marriage is Masai. Masai comes from Nishio in Japan where sixty per cent of all marriages are arranged. What does the expression 'arranged marriage' suggest to you?

Task 3

Read the multiple choice questions below and then listen to the conversation and choose the correct answers.

1 'Omiai' is the Japanese word for
- **a** a wedding.
- **b** people who marry.
- **c** an arranged marriage.
- **d** the wedding day.

2 The possible marriage partners exchange photographs
- **a** in a restaurant.
- **b** with a go-between.
- **c** of their families.
- **d** before they meet.

3 To meet twenty possible marriage partners is
- **a** impossible.
- **b** quite common.
- **c** unlikely.
- **d** preferable.

4 If the girl doesn't fall in love with the boy,
- **a** she must tell him face to face.
- **b** she can ask someone to do it.
- **c** her family will tell him.
- **d** he never finds out.

Task 4

The word 'they' appears in all the extracts below. What does it refer to?

- **a** *...they're all successful.*
- **b** *... they have to exchange their photographs.*
- **c** *...they might go to a restaurant ...*
- **d** *... they don't have to decide on the spot.*
- **e** *... They probably worry about her ...*

Listen to the cassette again and see if you were right.

Task 5

Masai claims that all arranged marriages are successful. Why do you think this is the case?

Task 6

Now listen to Äre Helbemäe talking about her grandmother. First of all, listen specifically for the following information:

- the place her grandmother came from
- the decade when she got married
- Äre's grandfather's occupation and what happened to him

Task 7

Only one of the following is an accurate statement. Which one is it?

a Äre was talking about her grandmother, who was happily married twice.
b Äre's grandmother and grandfather had an unsuccessful marriage.
c Äre's grandfather was her grandmother's second husband.
d Äre was three when her grandfather died.

Task 8

Äre's story is reproduced below. Cross out the hesitations, repetitions and other features of spoken English and correct the small errors.

My grandmother was the oldest sister of … I think there were three of them and at that that that time that was end of last last century, girls couldn't get married until, you know, the the older ones had been married and she she was rather choosy and couldn't find a husband and then the other girls said oh we want to get married and you are not married as yet and she said all right next man comes, I'll accept her—him. And, of course, I mean that story went round the village and a man came whom she really hated and asked for her hand and she had promised and they got married. They didn't have a very big wedding as far as I have heard, and after six months she she was so fed up with the husband she said she was going to get a divorce and, of course, that time to get a divorce in Estonia that must have been 1860s, but she she she got a divorce and married my grandfather, who was a forester and then they had two daughters, my mother and her sister. And then my grandfather, being a forester in Alodaguza which is a really big forest, and he went to the forest and a bear had woken up during the hibernation time and he had a real fight with the bear and was was injured and apparently fainted and was lying in the snow for a long time and got pneumonia and died. When my mother was three, I think.

LISTENING 2 Getting divorced

Task 1

Do you know the difference (if any) between the following geographical areas?

England	The British Isles
Britain	Great Britain and Northern Ireland
Great Britain	The United Kingdom

Task 2

On the cassette, a marriage counsellor discusses the divorce rate in the United Kingdom. On the left below are a number of words and expressions that you will hear. Match them with the definitions on the right.

1 *first and foremost*	**a** reasons for ending a marriage
2 *grounds for divorce*	**b** free legal help and advice
3 *irretrievable breakdown*	**c** the point at which a marriage has no chance of surviving
4 *Legal Aid*	**d** being married to more than one person at the same time
5 *bigamy*	**e** most important
6 *prolonged separation*	**f** living apart for a long time

Task 3

Listen to the cassette and look at the groups of words below. Mark any words in the lists that you hear.

marry	married	marriage	subject	subjects	subjected
cost	costs	costly	happy	happier	happiness
offend	offence	offended	separate	separated	separation
prolong	prolongs	prolonged	different	difference	differences

Task 4

Read the True or False exercise below. Then listen to the cassette again and tick (✓) the appropriate box.

		True	False
a	England has the highest divorce rate in Europe.		
b	It's very difficult to get a divorce in Britain.		
c	Before 1971, it was more difficult.		
d	There are no divorces in small towns and villages.		
e	In cities, people are more likely to know divorced people.		
f	People often blame their marriage partners for their general frustration.		
g	Second marriages are more successful than first ones.		

Task 5

The marriage counsellor is asked a number of questions beginning with the question 'why?' Below each question are two alternative answers. Which answer more accurately reflects the counsellor's opinions?

1 *Why are there so many divorces in Britain?*
- **a** It's easy to get a divorce.
- **b** Because of the number of breakdowns.

2 *Why don't women who are suffering tell anyone about their problems?*
- **a** They're scared.
- **b** They don't know any others with the same problems.

3 *Why are there fewer divorces in small towns?*
- **a** People get help from their neighbours.
- **b** No one wants neighbours to know their problems.

4 *Why do so many people want a divorce?*
- **a** To marry someone else.
- **b** The reasons are not usually simple to explain.

5 *Why is it so risky getting married in your teens?*
- **a** You may meet someone else.
- **b** People change a lot by their early twenties.

Task 6

/ə/

This phonetic symbol represents the sound we call 'schwa'. Look at the phonetic transcription of the words 'was' and 'the' in the dialogue below. Notice that they have a 'schwa' in some situations and not in others. Can you explain this?

Were you here at *the* beginning of *the* lesson? /ðə/

Yes, I *was*. /wɒz/

Where were you at *the* end? /ðiː/

I *was* in *the* canteen. / wəz/ðə/

Task 7

Locate the 'schwa' in the following words that you heard on the cassette.

offence bigamy nowadays obviously separation

Task 8

Read the introduction to the interview that you heard on the cassette. Mark the words that contain the 'schwa'.

More than thirty per cent of marriages in the United Kingdom end in divorce, the highest rate of any country in Europe. There are also more people who are separated from their husbands and wives than anywhere else. In addition, there are more people in the UK who live together without getting married than in any other country that keeps records of this kind.

Listen again to see if you were right.

SPEAKING Living together

Task 1

Describe the photograph of the married couple. Consider the following:

- their age
- descriptive words for their faces
- their clothes
- the room
- how long they have been married
- where they met
- whether they have children and grandchildren

To answer these questions, you need to use guesswork, make deductions or give your opinions. If you are certain about the deduction that you are making, you can express it like this:

They must be at least sixty, because ...

They must have a lot of grandchildren because ...

Task 2

Read the following three passages and make a note of the verbs and other expressions used to *report what people said*. Which passage relates to the photograph?

a The door opened and Ted walked in, calmly announcing that he had broken off his engagement with Martha. Avril was startled and hesitantly asked him what he had just said. Ted repeated it, turned on his heel and made to leave. Gregory stormed over from the window and angrily called him back. He pointed out that the wedding was due to take place the next week and demanded to know what he was expected to tell Aunt Edith.

b Gordon and Emily have been married for fifty years. Gordon smiled when he was asked how they had met. He began to tell me about a dance hall in Croydon. Emily broke in and reminded him that it wasn't in Croydon, it was in Purley. Gordon agreed that it wasn't in Croydon, but insisted that it wasn't in Purley, either.

c Seventeen-year-old film star Gloria Vega announced yesterday that she was planning to marry in September. When asked the name of the lucky man, she revealed only that he was Greek and was not involved in the film world. She denied that it was Stavros Iannides, the fifty-one-year-old oil tycoon and pleaded with reporters to let her have some peace and quiet on her honeymoon.

Task 3

Write down in dialogue form what was said in each passage.

Task 4

Where is each passage taken from? Choose a possible source from the list below.

- a gossip column
- an oil advertisement
- a short story
- a wedding announcement
- a film script
- a local newspaper report

Task 5

Discussion Hungarian film star Zsa Zsa Gabor admitted to having been married seven times, possibly more. Possibly unfairly, film stars have a reputation for marrying and divorcing at a higher rate than the rest of the population. Why do you think they bother to get married at all?

PERSON A

SECTION 1

1

2

a They were good and quick learners. They listened intently to what the more experienced workers told them and they quickly picked up how to operate the machines.

b They started as young hopefuls in a very competitive business and got their first assignments by sending photographs of themselves to a clothing designer.

c They arrived in the city with no money, no prospects and nowhere to go. After spending some time in hostels, they started living rough on the streets.

SECTION 2

1
- a fashion model
- a building worker
- an airline pilot
- a supermarket cashier
- a police officer

2 **Role A** You want to be an athlete
Role B You want to study architecture
Role C You want to study wildlife.

3

HOMELESS? NO MONEY?

We may be able to help you.
We can provide you with
*** temporary accommodation ***
*** food and clothing ***
*** part-time work ***
*** job opportunities ***

CENTRAL CRISIS CENTRE

PERSON B

SECTION 1

Photographs Ask your partner to study the three photographs. Open a discussion using these suggestions:

Describe/compare

- the young people
- the work that they do
- the way they look

Discuss

- how young people can become homeless
- whether this situation would arise in your country
- what you think the future holds for the different groups

If you are working with a group, encourage an individual to start a discussion. Invite other students to answer.

Passages Ask your partner or the group to read the three passages and to link the themes of the passages and the photographs. Invite comments on where the extracts may have been taken from.

SECTION 2

Now choose one of the following activities:

1 **Activity** Ask your partner or the group to choose one of the occupations listed below and say why they think they would be ideal for it, or why they are sure they would *not* be ideal for it.

- a fashion model
- a building worker
- an airline pilot
- a supermarket cashier
- a police officer

2 **Discussion (in pairs or groups)** Tell the group to imagine that they are applying for a scholarship to study abroad. They should describe the study they intend to follow, where they want to go and how they will spend the money. They can choose from these roles:

Role A You want to be an athlete
Role B You want to study architecture
Role C You want to study wildlife

3 **Discussion** Tell your partner or the group to look at the advertisement aimed at homeless people. Encourage them to discuss it by asking these questions:

a Where do you think the poster would appear?
b What kind of accommodation do you think the Crisis Centre can offer?
c Do you think homeless people can stay there permanently?

Street life

LISTENING 1 The crowded streets of London

Task 1

Write down all the words and expressions you know to describe a traffic jam.

Task 2

Imagine you were a traffic reporter on a local radio programme. Which of the following means of transport would you consider helpful?

walking	tram	aeroplane	boat
car	bicycle	train	elevated railway
taxi	helicopter	underground train	motorbike

Task 3

On the cassette is a conversation between a radio presenter and a traffic reporter. Before you listen, study the map of London.

Now listen to the cassette and circle the London locations which are mentioned in the traffic report. Which ones are not mentioned?

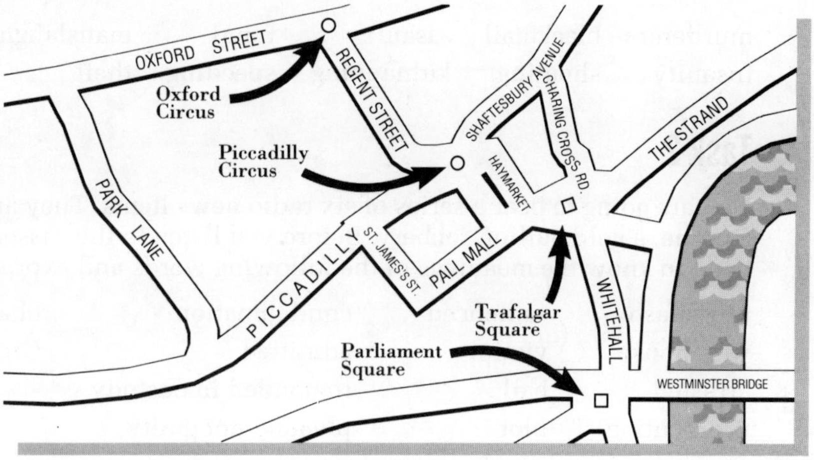

Task 4

According to the traffic report, the following problems are contributing to today's traffic situation in Central London. Before you listen to the cassette again, make sure you know what they mean:

- broken-down buses
- heavy congestion
- roadworks
- traffic lights out of order

Task 5

Now listen to the cassette again and match the traffic problems above to the locations below:

a Whitehall, Piccadilly, The Strand ____

b Pall Mall, St James Street, Trafalgar Square ____

c Haymarket, Charing Cross Road ____

d Shaftesbury Avenue, Regent Street, Oxford Street ____

Task 6

Read the extract from the traffic report below and mark the words you expect to be stressed.

Gerry What's causing all the hold-ups, Amy?

Amy There are just too many cars. And the weather's a problem. More people seem to be on the roads in their cars today because of the rain. I would suggest that anyone listening should come in by train or tube.

Gerry Good idea.

Now listen again to see if you were right.

Task 7

Traffic congestion is a problem in all major cities, and quite a lot of smaller towns and cities as well. What kind of problems are faced by the major cities in your country and what is being done to solve these problems?

LISTENING 2 The Salford gold bullion robbery

Task 1

Which of the following are crimes?

murderer	blackmail	assault	fraud	manslaughter	robber
insanity	shouting	kidnapping	speeding	theft	stealing

Task 2

You are going to hear a series of six radio news items. They are all about a crime, a gold bullion robbery. Before you listen to the cassette, you need to know the meanings of the following words and expressions:

newsflash	sentenced	condemnation	charged with
warehouse	victim	admitted	Crown Court
arrested	bail	remanded in custody	
prosecution	plot	pleaded not guilty	
counsel	proof	security vault	

Task 3

The six news items were broadcast on the radio over a period of time. Listen to the cassette. For item 1 decide when the crime took place. For items 2–6 decide how much time has passed since the **previous broadcast**.

Item 1 **a** Monday **b** Wednesday **c** Friday	**Item 2** It is now: **a** One week later **b** Two weeks later **c** Two months later	**Item 3** It is now: **a** The next day **b** Two days later **c** Three days later
Item 4 It is now: **a** Three weeks later **b** One month later **c** Three months later	**Item 5** It is now: **a** The same day **b** The next day **c** The following week	**Item 6** It is now: **a** Three days later **b** Three weeks later **c** Three months later

Task 4

Read the multiple choice exercise below. Try to answer the questions without listening to the cassette again.

1 The gold bullion was stolen from
- **a** a bank in Salford.
- **b** the Manchester police.
- **c** unknown robbers.
- **d** a warehouse near Manchester.

2 The arrested man was not
- **a** taken to court.
- **b** remanded in custory.
- **c** allowed to go home.
- **d** charged with robbery.

3 The man who was arrested
- **a** is probably a robber.
- **b** works for a security firm.
- **c** is in the building trade.
- **d** is a security contractor.

4 In a garage, the police discovered
- **a** Alan Michael Wigton.
- **b** part of the stolen goods.
- **c** the gold bullion.
- **d** the man who pleaded not guilty.

5 The defence counsel claimed that the police
- **a** could not prove that Wigton was the robber.
- **b** put the gold in Wigton's garage.
- **c** were victims of an elaborate plot.
- **d** had no idea how the bullion got there.

6 At the end of the trial, Wigton
- **a** was arrested with two other men.
- **b** admitted that he worked at the warehouse.
- **c** was sent to prison.
- **d** found £10,000 worth of the gold bullion.

Task 5

Regular past tense forms in English are pronounced in three different ways. Like this:

looked /t/ climbed /d/ started /ɪd/

Can you write down another three examples of each type?

Task 6

The following verbs appear on the cassette. Put them in the past tense and, if they are regular, add them to the lists you have started.

arrest	take	accuse	remand	admit	refuse
steal	discover	appear	reveal	sentence	find
plead	hide	charge	criticise	announce	name

Task 7

Choose six of the verbs above to complete the news broadcast below.

Today police _____ a man in connection with the bullion robbery at Salford Security Warehouse, which _____ place two weeks ago. The man, who has not been _____ , _____ in court this morning and was _____ with robbery. He was _____ in custody for three weeks.

Now listen again to see if you were right.

Task 8

Practise the pronunciation of the regular past tense forms by quoting the relevant phrases from the news item in Task 7.

SPEAKING Standstill

Task 1

Look at the photograph. Write down any words you can to describe it.

Task 2

What can you say for sure or imagine about the following in connection with the photograph?

a Where was the photograph taken? How do you know?
b What time of day is it?
c What kind of people are in the cars?
d Where do they live?
e Why do they make this kind of journey?
f How often do they do it?
g Is it worth it?

Task 3

Look at the three reading passages below. They are taken from three letters written to a newspaper on the subject of traffic in cities. Each passage does one of the following:

- suggests a cause for the problem
- criticises a transport decision
- suggests a solution to the problem

Read the extracts and decide which is which:

a Sir,

Without wishing to criticise the government's transport policy, may I offer the following plan for their consideration: make all commuting drivers stop at a point five miles from the centre of the city and take a bus from there.

b Sir,

The huge success of the car industry's advertising campaign is responsible for the terrible traffic situation. If we are allowed to continue buying as many cars as we do, it will not get any better.

c Sir,

The decision to raise the price of rail tickets by thirty per cent was an act of complete foolishness and whoever is responsible should be sacked.

Task 4

Group role-play What is the solution to the problem of too many cars in the centre of our cities? Here is your chance to tell the authorities what you think.

Divide the class into five groups. They will represent five different groups of people who have an interest in transport policy. The five groups are:

- city centre shopkeepers
- car manufacturers
- public transport users
- building contractors
- old people

In your group, discuss the traffic problem from the point of view of the group that you represent. Do shopkeepers like a lot of traffic in the centre of the city? Would car manufacturers react well to the banning of cars in cities? What do public transport users feel about people who drive into the city? How would building contractors benefit from government decisions about new roads? And how easy is it to get around the city centre if you're old?

After your group discussion, present your ideas to the rest of the class. See if you agree or disagree with the other groups.

The following expressions may be useful:

We think the government should …
Why don't they …
In our opinion …
From our point of view …
We suggest the following …
We recommend that the government should …

Exam practice: paper 4 LISTENING COMPREHENSION

FIRST PART

Fill in the end-of-term results.

	Classwork	Examination
English		
French		
Spanish		
History		
Geography		
Science		
Mathematics		
Art		

SECOND PART

Fill in the arrival and departure times and platforms.

	Departures	
To	**Time**	**Platform**
Bristol		
Liverpool	10.45	
Manchester		
Nottingham		1
Oxford		
Sheffield	10.05	

THIRD PART

For questions **1–6** match the functions and the descriptions.

THE X12 TELEPHONE SYSTEM

Function	**Description**
1 Call, Hold and Transfer	**a** You and a colleague can both speak to an incoming caller.
2 Intercom	**b** Incoming calls ring at every extension.
3 Three-Way Call	**c** You can talk to a number of other extensions at the same time.
4 Reminder Feature	**d** Automatic change to another extension.
5 Call Intercept	**e** Transfer to another extension without using switchboard.
6 Totalcall	**f** Noise made if all extensions are busy.

FOURTH PART

For questions **7–11** tick (✓) one of the boxes **A**, **B**, **C** or **D**.

7 The two speakers are

A tennis players.
B former tennis players.
C sports commentators.
D former sports commentators.

A	
B	
C	
D	

8 In the game they were watching,

A a British player was defeated by a German.
B a German player lost to a British player.
C a British player beat a German player.
D a British player won the match.

A	
B	
C	
D	

9 The loser was described as

A a left-handed German.
B a twenty-three-year-old barber.
C a marvellous left-hander.
D a Bristol man in his twenties.

A	
B	
C	
D	

10 The woman commentator was extremely critical of

A both players.
B the German.
C the British player.
D left-handers.

A	
B	
C	
D	

11 She thinks that British players

A lose confidence when things go wrong.
B are always looking for trouble.
C expect to lose.
D see the first sign of trouble very quickly.

A	
B	
C	
D	

12 Discussing the future, speculating and making predictions

What next?

LISTENING 1 The Intelligent House

Task 1

You are going to hear about some research into making houses more 'intelligent'. You will need to know the meaning of the following words and expressions:

gadget	burglars	sophisticated	city-dwellers
device	intruder	computerised	remote control
deter	commodities	heat-sensitive	

Task 2

On the left below is a list of modern 'gadgets' or 'devices'. Match them with the correct function on the right.

1 a burglar alarm
2 a central locking system
3 a thermostat
4 a fire alarm
5 an answering machine
6 a computerised phrasebook
7 a remote control
8 a fax machine
9 an electronic organiser

a takes telephone messages
b translates selected phrases into other languages
c switches on the television from ten metres away
d locks and unlocks car doors electronically
e photocopies a document via the telephone line
f stores information in a pocket-size computer
g makes a noise when a building is on fire
h controls the heating in a building
i makes a noise when a building is being broken into

Task 3

You will hear the following words on the cassette. As you listen, decide from the context which of the definitions below is the most likely.

1 *currently*
a today
b at the moment
c at the same time

2 *constant*
a faithful
b without stopping
c always the same

3 *particular*
a hard to please
b detail
c specific

4 *alerted*
a made aware
b scared
c warned

5 *thanks to*
a because of
b with compliments to
c in favour of

6 *shop around*
a visit many shops
b shop at different times
c look for the best prices

7 *prepared*
a cooked
b warned
c ready

Task 4

Read the True or False exercise below. Then listen to the cassette again and put a tick (✓) in the appropriate box.

	True	False
a Houses can do more than they could a hundred years ago.		
b The Intelligent House is the invention of one particular scientist.		
c Stephen Hall's invention will take photographs of burglars.		
d By 2020, most city-dwellers will live in Intelligent Houses.		
e An Intelligent House will know when to start cooking dinner.		
f In future, a house will be able to order and collect food from shops.		
g It will not be necessary to change the instructions if you change your mind.		
h Re-programming will be possible from abroad.		

Task 5

Below is a transcript of what scientist Stephen Hall said. Write it as a report, taking out hesitations and other aspects of spoken English.

Basically … er … today's … a house today doesn't do what people … what *busy* people want it to do … or rather, need it to do. Take … er … security, for example. I mean, a modern house isn't, you know, what you might call protected. All you have is … er … a simple device like a burglar alarm … someone opens the door, the front door and the … the alarm goes off and that's about it, really. I've designed a whole new … a completely new system of burglary prevention. If someone, a burglar, breaks into an intelligent house, a heat-sensitive camera, a mobile camera, will, you know, locate him, the burglar, and his picture will appear at a local crime prevention centre, a police station, in other words. And the burglar will only have to cough and the police will be able to find him on a computer. And the … um … the owner of the house will also carry a little … a little gadget … so he'll be alerted to the danger as well.

Task 6

The information about The Intelligent House that you have heard concentrates on two of the following topics. Which ones?

- home entertainment
- food
- cleaning
- using space efficiently
- security

Task 7

Discussion Would you like to live in an 'Intelligent House?'

Divide the class into two groups. One group should make a list of the advantages of an Intelligent House, the other group a list of the disadvantages. Then discuss your list with the other group.

Task 8

You heard all the following words on the cassette:

through *cough* *though* *enough* *bought*

Below are the five different phonetic transcriptons of the '-ough' part of each word. Match the words above with their phonetic symbols.

/ɔː/ /əʊ/ /ʌf/ /ɒf/ /uː/

Task 9

Listen to the cassette again to check the five pronunciations and write down three expressions that you hear that indicate that the discussion is about the *future*.

LISTENING 2 Journey to the End of Space

Task 1

Journey to the End of Space is a radio programme. What kind of programme could it be?

a comedy	a soap opera	a quiz programme
sports news	a historical drama	a futuristic adventure
pop music	a science programme	a chat show

Task 2

Which of the following characters could possibly appear in a programme called *Journey to the End of Space*? You can choose as many as you like but you must be able to justify your choices.

Batman	Sherlock Holmes	Darth Vader
Robin Hood	Superman	Mickey Mouse
Hamlet	Indiana Jones	James Bond

Task 3

Look at the list of words below.

greed	loan	tempt	go	pier
void	sleep	rest	way	loud

You can make a new word by adding the prefix sound /ə/ to all of these words. Example: pier > appear. You may need to change the spelling, but the pronunciation of the key word remains the same. Make a list of the new words. (There are two possibilities for the word 'loud'.)

Task 4

You should now have a list of twenty or twenty-one words, including the example. Listen to the cassette and tick (✓) the words in the list that you hear.

Task 5

Read the multiple choice questions below and then listen to the cassette again. Choose the correct answer.

1 The crew of the spaceship consisted of
a a female pilot and a female co-pilot.
b a male pilot and a female co-pilot.
c a female captain and an alien co-pilot.
d an alien captain and a female co-pilot.

2 At the beginning of the programme, the pilot was
a eating something nice.
b making a cake.
c attempting to eat something.
d in the middle of a delicious meal.

3 Dark tried to draw Jane's attention to
a what was on TV.
b the view out of the window.
c a photograph of some asteroids.
d an approaching problem.

4 Jane's immediate reaction was to
a tell Dark to wake up.
b explain the situation to the computer.
c shout at the top of her voice.
d ask for help from another member of the crew.

5 The computer was sympathetic but
a refused to help.
b went back to sleep.
c switched himself off.
d had no solution.

6 Jane decided to solve the problem by
a going to sleep.
b changing course.
c switching the computer on.
d ordering the compter to switch on.

7 To find out what happened next, we have to
a use our imagination.
b continue listening.
c listen to the next episode.
d answer a series of questions.

Task 6

The pilot's name is Jane /dʒeɪn/ Blake /bleɪk/. Listen to the cassette again and make a note of *five* words that rhyme exactly with *each* of her names.

Task 7

What happened next? Continue the drama of the sleeping computer, either in dialogue or prose form.

Task 8

Look at the misunderstanding in the following piece of dialogue:

Dark Look at the screen!

Jane What is it, Dark?

Dark It's the square thing in front of you, Captain.

'What is it?' is a question here which asks about the *problem*, not the screen. Think of some more dialogues like this. Here are some more starter lines:

I've got a problem with my car.
I need to go to a hospital.
You must let me use the telephone.
Oh no! Look at the clock!

SPEAKING UFOs

Task 1

Which of the following words and phrases would you use to describe the object in the picture?

foreign	spaceship	flying saucer
alien	aircraft	battleship
strange	rocket	supernatural

What does UFO stand for?

Task 2

In pairs, ask and answer the following questions:

a Where/ photograph/ taken?
b Who/ you/ think/ took/ it?
c Did/ he/ she/ intend/ take/ it?
d You/ think/ authentic?
e Could/ UFO/ fly/ close/ Earth/ without detection?

Task 3

If you saw a UFO, which of the following adjectives do you think would best describe the experience?

astonishing	exhausting	amusing	reminiscent
interesting	unusual	memorable	super
amazing	incredible	nice	disappointing
frightening	puzzling	unnerving	
different	unbelievable	rewarding	

Task 4

The following passages are about the existence of life on other planets. Decide which ones suggest a belief that there is life on other planets, and which do not.

a The likelihood of life existing on another planet is equivalent to the likelihood of the pieces of a wrecked aircraft being picked up by a hurricane and deposited, re-forming the original plane.

b If we think that there is no one up there … not a single living thing on any of the billion planets of the known universe … then we are very arrogant indeed.

c Life on Earth possibly originated in outer space. The originators must still be there.

d The position in the solar system that Earth occupies was an amazing accident, but an accident of such precision that no other planet in our solar system has even a blade of grass on it. This state of affairs will apply in other solar systems … but without the accident.

Which passages believe there *is* life on other planets? Which words and phrases if any, can you quote to support your argument?

Exam practice: paper 4 LISTENING COMPREHENSION

FIRST PART

For questions **1–5** tick (✓) one of the boxes, **A**, **B**, **C** or **D**.

1 The interviewee is

- **A** an expert on Moscow's problems.
- **B** pessimistic about the future.
- **C** involved in research into urban traffic problems.
- **D** concerned that there aren't enough cars.

2 By the year 2025,

- **A** there will be 125 more cars in cities.
- **B** the number of cars will increase by 125%.
- **C** the amount of city traffic will more than double.
- **D** Paris will have much more traffic.

3 The majority of cars in cities

- **A** contain fourteen per cent of the workforce.
- **B** are for public transport.
- **C** carry working people.
- **D** are official government cars.

4 People will decide to use their cars to travel into a city

- **A** when public transport improves.
- **B** because the city is too dangerous.
- **C** if it isn't too expensive.
- **D** because they are unhappy about public transport.

5 If car-users decide to use public transport again,

- **A** it may be too expensive.
- **B** they will be completely stupid.
- **C** there may not be enough capacity.
- **D** there will be the biggest traffic jam in history.

SECOND PART

Indicate the order in which the following topics are dealt with by the report. Put a tick (✓) if the writers of the report are in favour and a cross (✗) if they are against.

6 All-seater stadiums	
7 Barriers in stadiums	
8 Single-purpose stadiums	
9 Ground-sharing	
10 Artificial pitches	
11 New stadiums outside towns	

THIRD PART

For questions **12–17** tick (✓) whether the statements are true or false.

	Statement	True	False
12	Andy Cassidy is a modern musician.		
13	He thinks we will see more bands of different nationalities.		
14	At present, world music songs are often sung in English.		
15	The Gypsy Kings sing a Spanish dialect.		
16	Andy predicts that we will hear no more songs in English.		
17	There are some Japanese bands who are already very famous.		

FOURTH PART

Tick (✓) the correct boxes in this questionnaire.

LOCAL QUESTIONNAIRE

Local resident? Yes ☐ No ☐

Voted for which party?
Greens ☐ Social Democrats ☐ Conservatives ☐ Socialist Workers ☐

Voting intentions? Same ☐ Different ☐ Don't know ☐

Most important local issue?
Roads ☐ Old people ☐ Education ☐ Rubbish collection ☐

Children? No ☐ One ☐ More than one ☐

Most Important issue in Education?
More money ☐ New school buildings ☐ Smaller classes ☐

Introduction for teachers

Network Listening and Speaking is a source-book of practice material which can be used as a preparation for Papers Four and Five of the Cambridge First Certificate Examination.

It consists of twelve units, and a Starter Unit. The language areas covered by each unit (see contents) are the same as those covered by books 1 and 2. The topics are also the same, although they are dealt with in different units.

Each unit in the book is divided into three sections, consisting of the following: two listening comprehensions, plus exploitation material; a photograph and material for speaking activities based on it, reading material and role-play and discussion ideas. At the end of each unit you will find test material based on Papers Four and Five of the examination.

LISTENING section

Each of the listening texts is accompanied by the following:

- Pre-listening activities
  Example:
  Predicting what the subject-matter will be.
  What do you expect to hear?
  What do you already know about this subject?
  Make sure you know the meaning.

  (There are examples of all of these techniques in the Starter Unit).
- First-time listening activities
  Example:
  Listening for specific information.
  Listening for gist.
- Follow-up listening activities based on First Certificate examination exercises.
- Exercises based on a more detailed analysis of the text, listening and reading simultaneously.
  Example:
  Listening for missing words.
  Listening for extra words.
  Listening for different or wrong words.
- Pronunciation practice
  Example:
  Recognising particular sounds.
  Predicting stress and intonation patterns.
  Listening for missing endings of words.
- Where possible, there are suggestions for follow-up class discussions based on the listening texts.

There are examples of all these exercise types in the Starter Unit.

SPEAKING section

This section contains elements that are found in Paper Five, the Interview. Each unit contains the following:

- A photograph or photographs with material designed to exploit the different ways of talking about what you can see and what you can speculate about.
- Reading material. The main aim is to do the following:
  a to identify the *source* and the *subject-matter* of a reading passage.
  b to recognise the *intention*, i.e. why was the passage written and for whom?
- Role-play suggestions. The book concentrates on examining *character* and *motivation*. There are no long explanations of the past history of the character you have to play, or endless lists of things you have to do or say. When an actor plays a role, he or she asks these questions: why is the character in this situation and what are his or her motives?
- Discussion ideas.

There are examples of all these activities in the Starter Unit.

Examination practice section

Each unit (except the Starter Unit) has examination practice material written in the style of FCE Papers Four and Five. Odd number units (1–11) have four listening extracts, each with a FCE Paper Four activity. Even number units (2–10) have test material based on Paper Five. Unit Twelve has a final examination based on Paper Four and Paper Five.

Each Paper Four test should take about 40 minutes, which is twice as long as the real exam, so these sections can be done in two halves. Before each listening extract, give the students time to read the questions, then play the cassette once. Give them two minutes to work on the test, then play the cassette again.

With Paper Five tests, the photographic, reading and role-play material is on the right-hand page. The examiner's questions are on the reverse side. Encourage students to examine each other. One student should have the book open at the candidate's page, the other at the examiner's page.

UNIT 1 All in a day's work

This unit covers language used to **describe routine, habits and states**. The first listening extract is an interview with an Italian girl who is learning English in London. Note the unusual and brave methods she has and ask the class what they think about them.

The second listening extract is an interview with an English actress who appears in an Australian soap TV show. There is an opportunity to find out what the students think about this kind of entertainment, and how much they know about the programmes and characters that they have seen in their own countries.

The speaking section 'Women at work' consists of the following material:

- A photograph of women working in a factory.
- Reading passages about people's working lives.
- Role-play: Does your work give job satisfaction?

You will notice that all the subject-matter of Unit One concerns women.

Examination practice: paper 4

The Unit One examination items are about the following:

- Cinema listings: a telephone information service.
- Transport survey: an interview.
- Pet behaviour: a monologue.
- How computers work: an explanation.

UNIT 2 People and places

The language area for this unit is the language needed to **describe people and places**. The first listening extract is a telephone conversation between a bank employee and a man who wants to borrow some money. The description is of the man's work and domestic life. Ask the students to try to fill in more about Mr Sharp and his lifestyle and to speculate about the bank employee's report on him.

The second listening extract is a radio report about a new shopping centre. The report sounds suspiciously like a piece of free advertising for the centre! Ask the students to speculate how the owners of the centre arranged for the radio to do the piece about them.

The speaking section is called 'Lifestyles' and consists of the following:

- Photographs of two women and their families who live in very different circumstances.
- Descriptions of different people's lifestyles.
- A role-play based on one of these descriptions.

Examination practice: paper 5

The Unit Two examination consists of the following: Photographs and linked reading passages, discussion points and a cartoon.

UNIT 3 Each to his own

The language of **likes, dislikes, preferences and opinions** is examined in this unit. The first listening extract is an interview with a horror film fan. Warn students that John uses names of actors and directors, expecting that everyone will know who he is talking about.

The second listening extract is a series of radio advertisements for products which are named on the page. Do the radio advertisements in the students' own countries sound the same?

The speaking section starts off with a look at car advertising and ends with a role-play where a researcher interviews people about their reactions to TV car advertisements.

Examination practice: paper 4

The listening extracts in the examination sections are as follows:

- An advertisement for a fitness centre.
- Information about free gifts at a petrol station.
- A monologue about the price of great works of art.
- A radio show about pop music.

UNIT 4 Everything under the sun

The language area of this unit is **comparisons and contrasts**. This is one of the units where some of the material deals with environmental awareness. The usual environmental issues have been avoided, however. The first listening extract is a radio weather report. Although nothing on the page requires you to do this, you could lead this into a discussion on global warming and other climactic changes that have taken place. You may find that the students know a great deal about this from their other studies.

The second listening extract deals with the little-discussed pollution caused by noise, and is a documentary about the difficulties experienced by a woman who lived and worked in noisy environments.

The speaking section is entitled 'Environmentally-Friendly'? Using photographs and related passages, it looks at the claims of some products to be environmentally-friendly.

Examination practice: paper 5

The photos and other examination matter deal with the problem of litter.

UNIT 5 Working and learning

The language of **describing experience and skills** is dealt with in this unit. The first listening extract is a pre-recorded message from a telephone job service, used by people who want to find out about jobs. All the jobs which are discussed on this International Jobline require languages. What are the students planning to do with their language skills? Do they intend to work in a bilingual capacity, or in an English-speaking country? Which other languages, if any, are they learning?

The second listening extract is an interview with the principal of International House, London, one of the biggest private English language schools in England. Tony Duff grew up and was educated in Dublin, Ireland, which has an educational system which is very different from the British one. Is it similar to the system in the students' own countries?

The speaking section is about jobs, and the skills that are necessary to do particular things. There is a role-play activity (an interview for an unusual or dangerous job) and a discussion: Which is more important in a new job—experience or enthusiasm?

Examination practice: paper 4

The listening extracts in the examination are as follows:

- A monologue about the author Agatha Christie.
- A description of the amazing things insects can do.
- An application form to be filled in while listening.
- The world's most travelled people.

UNIT 6 Looking back

The main language skill dealt with here is **talking about the past**. The first listening extract is with an eighty-year-old woman who talks about her family and home in the early years of the 20th century. Although Mrs Williamson is very clear, there are some words and phrases that she uses that are quite old-fashioned and regional. Warn the students about this. The unusual words and phrases are all dealt with in the pre-listening and listening activities.

The second listening extract is a radio quiz where all the questions are about history. Warn the students that the exchanges between the contestants and the compère are very fast—it is a quiz, after all! Tell them simply to listen for the information requested in the exercises. With this extract, it is doubly important not to worry about words that they don't understand.

The speaking section deals with old houses and contains three extracts describing houses from very different novels. One is a literary English piece, one is from the Southern States of the USA and the third is from a Latin American novel.

Examination practice: paper 5

The examination practice section continues the theme of antiquity, with photographic material of old trains, cars and planes.

UNIT 7 Free time

Leisure time is the topic area of this unit and the language covers how to express **plans and intentions**. This is dealt with intensively in the second listening extract, an interview with a man who wants to organise a major arts festival in his village. Before that, there is an interview with a Samaritan. The Samaritans are a group of volunteers who help people who feel lonely, suicidal or depressed. This may be a sensitive area, so you should use your discretion about (a) listening to the extract and (b) opening up a discussion about the contents. The Samaritan who is interviewed is a very compassionate human being and dedicated to her work, which involves sitting by a telephone, often all night, in a Central London office and listening to people who are feeling desperate about their lives. To repeat, an interesting topic, but one where you must consider your students' own lives before you use it.

The second extract, the Millbrook Arts Festival, uses the language of plans and intentions but is really about dreams and aspirations. Ask the students to consider Mr Field's chances of success.

The title of the speaking section is 'Winners and losers' and continues the theme of leisure time through the topic of professional and Olympic sport.

Examination practice: paper 4

The listening extracts are as follows:

- An interview with a soccer manager.
- A list of messages on an answering machine.
- The proposed changes to a city council budget.
- An interview with a round-the-world cyclist.

UNIT 8 Getting away from it all

This unit continues the theme of leisure time, combining the topics of travel and tourism with language work on **advice, warnings and instructions**. The first listening extract is a safety announcement on an aeroplane. Before you play this, find out how many people in the class have flown and get them to write down as many things as they can remember from the safety instructions. If you have time, invite the class in pairs or groups to put together a safety announcement in English.

The second extract is taken from a radio phone-in programme. When the BBC had a monopoly of broadcasting in the United Kingdom (about 25 years ago), there was no such thing as a phone-in programme on the radio. Now, with a large number of local commercial stations and local BBC stations, most radio stations have phone-ins as an important element of their output. Is this the same in the students' countries? The phone-in featured in the extract is a holiday advice programme, where listeners give advice based on their own holiday experiences.

The speaking section continues the theme of airline safety instructions.

Examination practice: paper 5

The photographic and other material in the examination section continues the theme of holidays.

UNIT 9 Keeping fit and eating right

The language developed is that needed to express **obligation, necessity, permission and prohibition**. Unit Four dealt with the environment and now Unit Nine looks at how people treat their own bodies. The listening extracts concern food and sport. The first deals with an American football team in England. American football is becoming more and more popular in Europe and other areas outside the USA. Do the students know anything about it? Do they like it?

The second extract is a heated argument between three people who disagree about what is the best way to eat healthily. Tell the students that this will be one of the more difficult extracts they have heard, partly because of the argument, and partly because the people speaking all know each other.

The overall theme of this unit is how we look after our bodies, how well we eat and the exercise we take. Encourage the students to say what they do to keep fit and healthy, and what they know about healthy eating and the problems of poor diet. They may know something about this from their other studies.

The speaking section is about cadet training and military service. The boys who are featured in the American football piece used to train as army cadets when they were still at school. Cadet military training is a very contentious issue in the UK, as is the whole subject of military or community service. Again, it may be a sensitive issue, but there is great scope for class discussion about this topic if the class wants to talk about it.

Examination practice: paper 4

The listening extracts are as follows:

- Some information about school visits.
- An explanation of the pricing policy of an airline.
- An interview with an actress about going to drama school.
- An informative piece about guide dogs for the blind.

UNIT 10 Relationships

This unit deals with the language needed to **report events and express opinions**. The topics dealt with are marriage and divorce. Even if the second extract, a discussion of divorce statistics, seems a problematic theme for your students, you will find the information in the first part informative and entertaining. Listening 1 contains interviews with two women, one from Japan and the other from Estonia. Masai from Japan talks about *omiai*—Japanese arranged marriages. In some Japanese cities, more than half of all marriages are arranged through agencies and go-betweens. Masai is very insistent that it is a good system. What do your students think? The second interview, with Äre Helbemäe from Estonia, tells an amazing story about her grandmother's marriage.

The divorce extract may deal with a sensitive issue but Listening 2 contains some surprising information if you think your students would be interested and not offended by the subject-matter.

The speaking section continues the themes of relationships, marriage and divorce and ends with a discussion about multiple marriage. Again, if this is a sensitive issue with some of your students, it may be better to avoid too much discussion of the contents.

Examination practice: paper 5

The examination practice focuses on young people, their problems and ambitions.

UNIT 11 Street Life

Cause and reason, explaining and criticising are the language areas covered in this unit. The topics are crime and traffic. The first listening extract may be difficult for two reasons. Firstly, it is a report by a radio traffic reporter speaking from inside a helicopter and secondly, it refers to a large number of places in Central London. If you look in the book, you will see that most of the place names are famous London landmarks. It is recommended that you spend some time on this map before you listen to the extract. Ask the students if they have ever visited London, and if they can identify any famous places in the map area—the Houses of Parliament, Nelson's Column, etc. Explain to the class that the extract will be a bit difficult because of the extraneous noise of the helicopter. They should be able to do the exercises without serious problems even if they don't understand everything that they hear.

The second extract is a series of radio reports about a gold bullion robbery. The reports deal with events lasting for some months, and students have to listen carefully to the time sequence.

The speaking section continues the topic of traffic, with photographic material, letters to newspapers and a role-play activity dealing with urban traffic chaos.

Examination practice: paper 4

The listening extracts are as follows:

- An interview between an teacher and a parent.
- A railway departures announcement at a railway station.
- A salesman talking about a multi-function phone.
- A radio tennis commentary.

UNIT 12 What next?

The topic is science and technology and the unit covers language needed for **speculating and making predictions**. The first listening extract is an alarming piece, entitled 'The Intelligent House', about the kind of houses we may inhabit in the 21st century. The expression 'intelligent house' is used to describe the technological developments that will revolutionize domestic life. Ask the students what they think the expression 'intelligent house' could possibly mean, and encourage them to talk about anything they have learnt or read about it.

The final listening extract in the book (except for those in the final examination practice) is a light-hearted piece of comic radio drama called 'Journey to the End of Space'. It has been written to offer the possibility of some useful follow-up work, particularly pronunciation practice, but the students should listen to it first and foremost as an entertainment, a reward for having reached the end of the book.

The speaking section deals with the subject of UFOs—unidentified flying objects, or flying saucers, as they used to be called in English. What similar expressions exist in the students' own languages to describe what are always presumed to be alien spacecraft (if they exist)? What stories do the students know about UFOs, and do they believe in them? This is a topic which usually arouses a lot of interest and free conversation, and you must decide how 'free' it should be, because it could go on for a long time!

Further discussion ideas on the 21st century e.g. space travel, other worlds, medicine, new sport and leisure activities. Discussion in groups.

Examination practice: paper 4

The listening extracts are as follows:

- A discussion about future urban traffic problems.
- A report on sports stadiums in the future.
- A radio interview about future pop music trends.
- An opinion poll interview about future voting intentions.

Answer key

Starter unit

LISTENING

Task 3

a No. The inspector introduced himself and she didn't know why he had come.

b Catherine Parker, the shop manager.

Task 4

aF **b**T **c**T **d**F **e**T **f**F

Task 5

2

Task 6

Inspector Are you the owner of this shop? ↗
Mrs Carter Yes, I am.
Inspector And were you here yesterday? ↗
Mrs Carter Yes.
Inspector Can you tell me what time you arrived? ↗
Mrs Carter Yes, but why do you want to know? ↘
Inspector Just a routine enquiry, Mrs Carter. What time did you arrive? ↘
Mrs Carter About 9.30.
Inspector And what time did you leave? ↘

Task 7

Mrs Carter I stayed until ʎ midday.
Inspector I see. ʎ You weren't here in the afternoon?
Mrs Carter No. What is ʎ this about?
Inspector Was anybody here?
Mrs Carter Inspector, you ʎ must tell me why you're asking all these questions.
Inspector There was a robbery at Milton's Bank yesterday ʎ. The people ʎ left the bank … and disappeared.

Task 8

/æ/ back bank man pack manager contacting
/ɑː/ asking afternoon Parker
neither: that (weak form) address arrived woman Friday anybody can (weak form)

Task 11

Neil Armstrong Buzz Aldrin Cape Kennedy Michael Collins

Task 12

1c **2**d **3**b **4**a **5**d

Task 14

The journey ~~only~~ lasted for four days. Finally, Apollo went into orbit around the moon. Collins remained ~~alone~~ in the spacecraft, and the other two descended to the moon's surface ~~together~~ in a ~~much~~ smaller craft, the lunar module. After a moment of ~~high~~ drama, when the two astronauts narrowly avoided landing in a ~~deep~~ crater, the lunar module finally reached its destination.

Task 15

So, on July 21st, Armstrong ~~began~~ the first person to set ~~food~~ on the moon. His first ~~works~~, as he stood on the ~~moon~~ surface, were these: 'That's one small ~~stop~~ for a man, one giant ~~leak~~ for mankind.'

Task 16

Armstrong and Aldrin collect sample of dust and rot and took photograph before return to Apollo for the return journal to Earth.

Task 17

Armstrong Collins apollo one module rock

Reading passages

1 Extracts a and c
2 a is a newspaper review
c is an advertisement
3 'Aliens' refers to people not from a particular country. It is not a letter to a newspaper. It refers to 'one of your immigration officers'.

Exam practice

1a **2**c **3**b

Unit 1

LISTENING 1

Task 2

Listening	—
Speaking	✓
Pronunciation	✗
Grammar	✗
Reading	✓
Writing	✓
Spelling	—

Task 3 (Suggested answer)

Sometimes it's quite difficult to meet English people and practise the language, so the way I practise my English is by watching TV most of the time or sometimes when I'm walking in the street, I stop people with English-looking faces and I say 'I'm sorry, what time is it please?' Then they tell me the time. Or if you appear a bit lost in the street, English people are very helpful. They come to you and ask if they can help. I say: 'Yes, please! I'm really lost and I don't know where this place is.' That way you just start a conversation, it's a good way of practising the language.

Task 4

Reading and writing. ∧ I … I read quite a lot and ∧ I read more in English than Italian now and I've got to start picking up Italian books ∧ … um I … I read lots of newspapers you know from the gossipy ones to the ∧ intellectual ones. ∧ I do like writing er when I've got time, I always ∧ keep in touch with friend. I'm quite confident about my writing because I ∧ studied quite a lot at school and they've given me a very good basis and I'm very confident ∧ in my spelling.

Task 5

/ɪ/ English illogical middle skills listening irregular

/iː/ please speaking people reading TV street

LISTENING 2

Task 3

4.45 am	*Alarm call*
5.00 am	*Get up*
5.45 am	*Studio car arrives*
6.00 am	*Arrive at studio*
6.30 am	*Make-up Department*
7.30 am	*Script meeting*
8.30 am	*On the set*

Task 4

aF **b**T **c**T **d**T **e**T **f**F **g**F

Task 5

Interviewer What do the people who live in the actual street think about all this filming at night? ↘
Celia What do you mean … the people in the street? ↘
Interviewer The residents of Carey Street, or whatever the real name is. ↘
Celia It isn't a real street. ↘
Interviewer What? ↗
Celia It isn't a real street! ↘
Interviewer Not a real street? ↗
Celia No! I thought everybody knew that! ↘
Interviewer I didn't! I thought it was a real street! ↘
Celia No … it's a studio set! It's in the car-park behind the TV studio! ↘
Interviewer It must be enormous! ↘
Celia What? ↘
Interviewer The car-park. ↘
Celia Why? ↘

Task 7

I play a young English girl called Elizabeth who has just arrived in the local neighbourhood. Her family has recently emigrated from England and almost everything is very different. She sort of spends most of her time getting things completely wrong because she simply doesn't understand what people are saying to her, or she doesn't understand how the money works. She initially goes to the local high school, which is really very different from the school she originally went to in England.

Most of the extra words are adverbs.

Task 8

every day
daily routine
usually
what time do you get up?
do you go out in the evening?

SPEAKING

Task 4

a a computer operator
b a factory worker
c a firefighter

Task 5

on average
seven hours a day
spends the evening
I'm on call for between eight and twelve hours a day
almost all the time

Exam practice

FIRST PART

Odeon	One	Two	Three	Four	Five
Monday–Thursday	*A*	E	D	*B*	C
Friday–Sunday	B			A	
Late-night Friday + Saturday	*C*	*A*	*E*	B	*D*

SECOND PART

PUBLIC TRANSPORT SURVEY

a Public transport used
- [x] every weekday
- [ ] regularly at weekend
- [ ] occasionally at weekend
- [x] rarely at weekend

b Purpose of weekday travel
- [x] work [ ] leisure [ ] other

c Destination
- [x] central area [ ] suburban area

d Time of morning journey
- [ ] before 8.00 [ ] 8–8.15 [ ] 8.15–8.30
- [x] 8.30–8.45 [ ] 8.45–9.00 [ ] after 9.00

e Length of morning journey
- [ ] Less than 20 minutes [x] More than 20 minutes

f Time of evening journey
- [ ] 4.30–5.00 [x] 5.00–5.30 [ ] 5.30–6.00

g Season ticket?
- [ ] Yes [x] No

THIRD PART

1T **2**F **3**F **4**T **5**F **6**F

FOURTH PART

7c **8**a **9**d **10**d **11**c **12**b

Unit 2

LISTENING 1

Task 3

aF **b**F **c**T **d**F **e**T **f**T **g**T

Task 4

LOAN APPLICATION FORM

Name *Peter Sharp*

Address *27 Petley Lane*

Occupation *Production Controller*

How long in this employment for?
Temporary [ ] Permanent [ ] Trial [x]

Married Yes [x] No [ ] **Children** Yes [ ] No [x]

Accommodation House [ ] Flat [x] Other [ ] Rented [ ] Owned [ ]

Smoker [x] Non-smoker [ ]

Task 5

Archer What do you do, Mr Sharp?
Sharp I'm ʌ production control at a computer assembly plan.
Archer And how much do you learn?
Sharp About six hundred ʌ a month, after tasks.
Archer How long have you been walking at the plan, Mr Sharp?
Sharp A week.
Archer ʌ Is it a permanent partition?
Sharp I'm on a month ʌ try. Depends on that, I may gate a permanent chop.

Task 6

/tʃ/ Chelsea children future
/ʃ/ production sure shop position shall

LISTENING 2

Task 3

1a **2**b **3**b **4**d **5**b

Task 4

Blandsmere Shopping Centre Ground Floor Plan

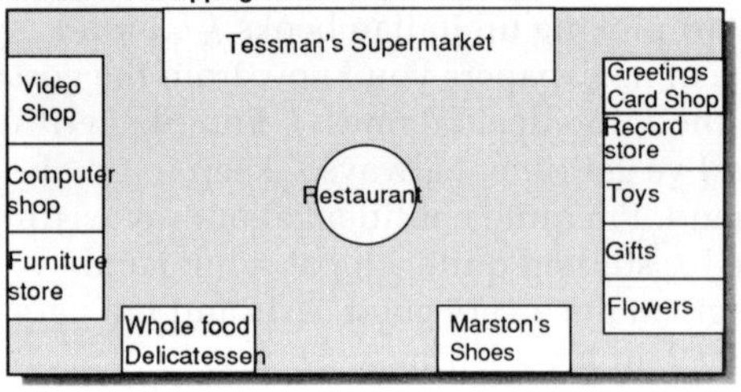

Blandsmere Shopping Centre Upper Floor Plan

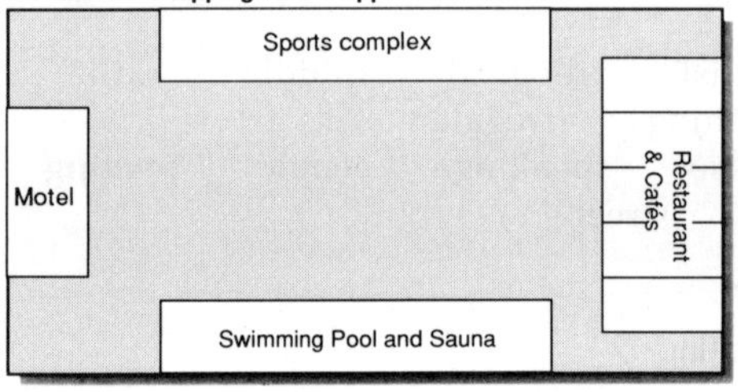

Task 5

I'm standing ʌ in the middle of the ground floor of the ʌ Blandsmere Shopping Centre in Croydon, about fifteen miles from ʌ London. It's a huge indoor complex, with an extraordinary variety of shops and a large ʌ restaurant here in the middle.

ʌ In front of me, I can see Tessmann's Supermarket, the biggest ʌ I've ever seen. That takes up ʌ the north side of the square. On my left, on the west side of the square, there are ʌ shops … a video market and a furniture store. On my right ʌ are a series of smaller shops. I can see a greetings ʌ shop, next to that a record store … and more shops selling toys ʌ and flowers.

SPEAKING

Task 3

a a short story **b** a letter **c** an advertisement

Task 4

b and **c**

Task 5

a never **b** I only work afternoons
c Helen is living … in one room

Exam practice

Section 1
1c 2b 3a

Unit 3

LISTENING 1

Task 3

Actors: Christopher Lee Vincent Price Peter Lorre Bela Lugosi Peter Cushing Jack Nicholson Boris Karloff
Director: Roger Corman
Writer: Edgar Allan Poe

Task 4

aT bF cF dF eF

Task 5

They all use this ~~idea of a~~ house on a hill in a storm or in a ~~dark~~ forest or somewhere out of the way where you are ~~completely~~ isolated. I think that's why Psycho is so ~~totally~~ memorable as well because it's an isolated place and the image of the ~~mysterious~~ house on the hill. People can imagine themselves being there and ~~actually~~ being in that situation. They never have ~~anything like~~ telephones and the electricity never works and there's always ~~going to be~~ a cellar. It's the darkness that's in all of us.

LISTENING 2

Task 2

1c 2c 3a 4c 5d 6b

Task 3

No one likes to come home ~~late~~ and find that their house has been ransacked. It's even worse when you know they got in ~~only~~ because your doors and windows weren't securely locked. Do the ~~really~~ sensible thing … fit Securex locks to all your doors and windows. Securex locks ~~really~~ protect from unwelcome visitors. So … fit Securex … before ~~you find~~ it's too late.

Sally Richards talks about the *Sunday Post*:

I ~~really~~ love it … it's got ~~absolutely~~ everything I could possibly want in a Sunday newspaper. ~~I think~~ I'd rather read the *Sunday Post* than ~~almost~~ anything else. Yes … you could ~~almost~~ say I prefer the *Sunday Post*!

Sally Richards ~~usually~~ reads the *Sunday Post*. Read it on Sunday and you could ~~possibly~~ win an exciting holiday for two in ~~sunny~~ Madagascar. The *Sunday Post*. ~~Try to~~ read it.

Task 4

/s/ thinks peace else works carpets likes
/z/ clothes pairs needs sales doors vitamins Richards housewives business curtains

SPEAKING

Task 4

a an advertisement
b a newspaper article
c a letter to the manufacturer
Opinion words: speaking personally in my opinion

Exam practice

FIRST PART

sauna swimming pool gymnasium
vegetarian restaurant
personal training programme
light and airy studios

SECOND PART

1 750 coupons or 500 coupons and £25
2 500 or 400 and £10
3 500 or 200 and £30
4 600 or 300 and £30
5 200 or 100 and £10
6 100 coupons
7 10 coupons

THIRD PART

8c 9b 10b 11a 12c 13b

FOURTH PART

	Rob	Anna	Steve
Penny Lane *(The Beatles)*	✗	✗	✓
Sympathy for the Devil *(The Rolling Stones)*	✗	✓	✗
Pinball Wizard *(The Who)*	✗	✓	✓

Unit 4

LISTENING 1

Task 2

'Foggy' has no symbol

Task 3

	6 am	Midday
Northern Ireland and Scotland	6°C	12°C
Wales and Northern England	10–12°C	
South West and Central England	cool	
South East England and East Anglia	fog 12°C	

Task 4

aF **b**F **c**T **d**F **e**T

Task 5

Here is the weather forecast for Great Britain and Northern Ireland for tomorrow, Tuesday the fourth of August. First of all, the forecast for six o'clock in the morning.

In Northern Ireland and Scotland, it will be cloudy with occasional showers. Winds will be light and from the north east and there will be mist in sheltered areas. Temperatures will be around six Celsius.

In Wales and Northern England, it will be cloudy with more showers and occasional bright intervals. Winds will be from the south west and temperatures will be higher than the seasonal average at around ten to twelve Celsius.

Task 6

By midday tomorrow, the picture will be quite different. Northern Ireland and Scotland will be mainly sunny with temperatures of twelve degrees Celsius, although a strong east wind will make it seem cooler. Wales and Northern England will experience much heavier rain and cooler temperatures than the rest of the country, with much stronger winds from the south east.

In South West and Central England, the wet and windy start will give way to much warmer weather due to a warm breeze coming from the south east, with occasional bright spells and sunshine. In the South East and East Anglia, expect occasional thunderstorms and heavy rain. Temperatures in this area will be about average.

All in all, a pretty normal day for the weather.

LISTENING 2

Task 3

aT **b**T **c**F **d**F **e**T **f**F **g**F **h**T

Task 4

1c **2**b **3**a **4**b **5**a

Task 5

Interviewer Today we ⋏ focus ⋏ on the problem of noise, noise at home and noise at work. Medical expert ⋏ agree that there are definite link ⋏ between noise and stress level ⋏ … the noisy ⋏ the environment, the more stress you are like ⋏ to experience. And it's even worse when a person is force ⋏ to live and work in noise ⋏ environment ⋏ . This seem ⋏ to have been the problem for Ann Dickinson.

Ann … the first place I live ⋏ in when I move ⋏ here was real ⋏ lousy. It was on a main road … I was used to living out in the country. There were lorry ⋏ passing by the front door all day and all night. Then the local council put a ban on truck ⋏ using that road during the night, so thing ⋏ got marginal ⋏ better and I got a bit more sleep. But then I decide ⋏ to move and thing ⋏ got much worse …

SPEAKING

Task 3

a milk **b** hair-spray **c** paper

Task 4

a advice **b** news item **c** criticism

Exam practice

1c **2**a **3**b

Unit 5

LISTENING 1

Task 3

	Position	Location	Languages Required	Salary
1	Personal secretary	Paris	German, Italian, Greek, Spanish	12,000 francs per month
2	Interpreter	Brussels	English, French, Dutch	60,000 Belgian francs
3	Translator	Athens	Greek & Italian	Fees

Task 4

The second job we are offering today is based at the European Commission building in Brussels. It's for an interpreter who can speak English, French and Dutch and who has experience of simultaneous translation work. The starting salary is 60,000 Belgian francs per month. All reasonable removal expenses will be paid and assistance will be given in finding accommodation in Brussels.

Task 5

/ɜː/ service interpreters first working personal third

LISTENING 2

Task 2

dominated primary comprehensive national compulsory college sacrifice academic

Task 3

3

Task 4

1b 2b 3a 4c 5d 6c 7b

Task 5 (suggested answer)

Before that, I had been at a primary school, what in Ireland in those days was called a national school. You didn't actually pay for it so I had the experience of going from a very posh infant school which was run by nuns to this national school where the social context was completely different from what I'd come from and then to this rather posh secondary school.

Task 6

Ken And would you call it a comprehensive system, as we call it in Britain?

Tony No, absolutely not a comprehensive system. I mean, that's where it is completely different. In addition to being dominated by the church until 1966, I think, virtually all education in Ireland was private, you had to pay for it. That's why I mentioned this national school I went to. There you didn't pay but everybody only had compulsory and state provided education to the age of twelve. That did change in '66 but the generation that I came from was very much brought up … er … on the idea that you had to pay for education and parents would save in order to provide children with a secondary school opportunity. In that respect, it's very like certain countries in Europe where parents work hard specially to provide education for their children so … no, it's not at all a comprehensive system. Not at all.

SPEAKING

Task 5

1c 2a 3b

Task 6

a a policeman **b** a pilot **c** a housing officer

Exam practice

FIRST PART

1b 2d 3c 4d 5c 6c

SECOND PART

7F 8F 9T 10T 11F 12T 13F

THIRD PART

APPLICATION FORM

Full name Michael John TRUELOVE

Address 26 RUDLAND Square, Reading

A-levels English, German and RUSSIAN

Degree in Russian and GERMAN

From BRUNEL University

Languages spoken 1.Russian 2.German 3.French 4.SWEDISH

Fluency 1.Fluent 2.FLUENT 3.Average 4. ELEMENTARY

Business qualifications MBA ☐ Yes ☑ No

Word processing ☐ Yes ☑ No

FOURTH PART

Park Thompson of Ohio USA and Giorgio Ricatto of Turin, Italy are the world's most travelled men. They have both visited all 170 of the world's sovereign states.

David Kunst, an American, walked round the world between June 1970 and October 1974.

Tomas Carlos Pereira from Argentina spent ten years walking 48,000 kilometres around five continents.

John Lees from Brighton holds the record for the fastest walk across the USA.

Unit 6

LISTENING 1

Task 2

a impossible **b** possible **c** possible **d** possible **e** impossible

Task 3

1d 2b 3d 4d 5b 6c 7b

Task 4

1c 2c 3b 4a

Task 5

Nellie I went to St Ambrose school, chair school, where we had to go to church every Friday mourning. We weren't aloud in church without a cat and so there was always a fire between my sisters and myself to find a cat.

Ken Tell me something about the way, for example, that houses were eaten. What did you do for eating?

Nellie With a cold fire. We used to have the cold delivered in the stream and we had grids in the street where the cold went down into the seller and it was our John when we came home from school to shuffle all this cold into the seller.

LISTENING 2

Task 3

Shirley 7 Michael 4 Christine 3

Task 4

1 George Washington
2 1789
3 1865
4 Dallas, Texas
5 Neil Armstrong
6 Corsica
7 1805
8 He wanted to unify Italy
9 Das Kapital
10 Trier, Germany
11 Mahatma Gandhi
12 The attack on Pearl Harbor
13 December 7th 1941
14 Mao Tse Tung

Task 6

a2 **b**4 **c**6 **d**5 **e**7 **f**1 **g**3

Task 7

/ɜː/ first earth thirty
/aɪ/ designed Chinese five United
/ɪ/ listeners India fingers quiz think fifteen history Italy

SPEAKING

Task 3

a the southern USA **b** London, England
c Latin America

Task 4

a a and c **b** gloomy **c** damaged by rain
d there's a porch **e** reader should choose

Exam practice

1a **2**b **3**c

Unit 7

LISTENING 1

Task 2

- lonely or depressed people
- a few hours each week, plus one overnight shift once a month
- one hundred

Task 3

1b **2**a **3**b **4**b **5**a

Task 4

I think we live in a society that moves very quickly and ∧ doesn't find ∧ time for people who can't match up to the pressures that are put on them. It's ∧ for people who are without support at a ∧ stressful time and it's often there for people who ∧ have support and ∧ friends they could talk to but it's something very private that they'd rather take elsewhere ∧ to someone objective. So the service offers something which is always there … it' ∧ befriending without questioning ∧ , it's completely confidential, you'll find a warm response, ∧ someone there to listen to whatever you say, whatever the problem is. They won't be shocked or ∧ bored, ∧ you'll have their full attention and care and I think it's ∧ something that we don't always find ∧ .

LISTENING 2

Task 3

1b **2**a **3**b **4**b **5**a

Task 5

1a **2**a **3**c **4**d **5**c **6**b **7**d

Task 6

And now some local news. The village of Millbrook, which is about thirty miles south of Bristol, is not somewhere that you immediately associate with the arts. There are no cinemas or theatres there, and no auditorium where you could put on a concert. But there is a big new conference centre and one local resident has decided that he would like to organise an arts festival there. Sarah Thompson went to see how he was getting on.

Task 7

Millbrook has three thousand inhabitants, two churches, three pubs, a restaurant and a large conference centre, which opened about two years ago. Some of the villagers were a bit put out by the conference centre, which has led to a big increase in traffic through the village. One particular resident, however, has decided that the conference centre presents the village with a golden opportunity. The resident is Mr Rupert Field. Mr Field, what gave you the idea of holding an arts festival at the conference centre?

SPEAKING

Task 2

a spoken **b** spoken **c** written

Task 3

a5 **b**6 **c**2

Exam practice

FIRST PART

Team: O'Toole Hunt Smith Bradley Racket Cross Purvis Burton Rowe Matthews Henry

Subs: Barton Higgins

SECOND PART

Appointment with Mr Shilton on Thursday at 4 pm
Choir Practice on Thursday at 4 pm.
Exhibition of Welsh artists on Thursday evening.
Dinner with Angela on Friday
Game of squash with Paul on Thursday at 6 pm
Parents' visit on Sunday afternoon
Lunch with Jonathan on Sunday

THIRD PART

Item	Current year	Next year
Education	12 million	*12 million*
Social Services	4 million	*3 million*
Lighting, cleaning	½ million	*½ million*
Leisure and recreation	3 million	*2 million*
Housing	6 million	*3 million*
Police	3 million	*4 million*
Ethnic minorities	½ million	*½ million*
Administration	5 million	*6 million*
TOTALS	**34 MILLION**	**31 MILLION**

FOURTH PART

1b 2c 3d 4c 5a 6a 7b

Unit 8

LISTENING 1

Task 1

c e a g b f d h

Task 4

high-heeled shoes straps seat pocket
life-jacket permitted emergency unlikely aisles

Task 5

a3 b6 c1 d5 e2 f4

Task 6

remove: take off *extinguish:* put out
inflate: blow up

Task 7

For your information and safety, please read the safety instruction booklet in the seat pocket in front of you. And now, in preparation for take-off, please make sure that your seat-belt is securely fastened, you seat is in the upright position and the table in front of you is folded away.

LISTENING 2

Task 1

1c 2b 3b

Task 2

1f 2a 6d

Task 3

1b 2b 3b

Task 4

Gerry What are you going to tell us about, Tim? ↗
Tim Paradors. ↘
Gerry What? ↗
Tim Paradors. ↘
Gerry What are paradors? ↘
Tim Accommodation for tourists in Spain. ↘
Gerry You mean hotels? ↗
Tim No, they're not hotels. ↘
Gerry What are they, then? ↘

Task 5

/θ/ thanks nothing thought north south Bournemouth
/ð/ the those that there they them

Exam practice

1a 2c 3b

Unit 9

LISTENING 1

Task 3

aF bF cF dT eT fF gF hT

Task 4

Toby There aren't any t(2) near where we l(1). We had to travel about twenty miles to find one. And it wasn't e(2) to get into the t(2). They make sure that you're really i(1). And then you have to wait w(2) before they decide i(1) they want you to join.
Adam That's right, but I t(1) they were p(1) p(2) to s(2) us because we're both quite b(1) and strong, but we also know the rules. They have a lot of d(1) w(1) some of the new players because the rules can be a b(1) c(1).

LISTENING 2

Task 2

cut down on/ reduce the amount of/ eat less
eaten/consumed/taken
rubbish/nonsense/ridiculous

Task 3

a Alan, Linda, Brenda
b they disagree with each other

Task 4

a Linda **b** Alan **e** Brenda

Task 5

1d 2c 3b 4d 5a 6a 7c 8b

Task 6

Brenda So what's your advise to people who want to dye it?
Alan I think that the most important thing to tell people who won't to lose wait is this: you've got to eat less. There is simply no other weigh.
Brenda I don't agree.
Alan Listen, Brenda ... most people who are overweight heat too much. The sensible thing to tell them is that they've got to cat down on what they eat.
Brenda No, I'm sorry, Alan, I think you're quiet wrong. People should eat a balanced diet of good food.
Alan Yes?
Brenda It isn't necessary to eat last. It's simply necessary to eat will.

SPEAKING

Task 5

a permission **b** prohibition **c** obligation

Exam practice

FIRST PART

	Visit one	Visit two	Visit three	Visit four
Country	Italy	Spain	USA	Switzerland
When?	February	Easter	Easter	May
Cost	£240	£200	£210	£70
Deposit by	Nov 28th	Oct 31st	Jan30th	End of February
Number of places	60	60	16	50

SECOND PART

From Edinburgh Departing	New York or Miami Returning		
	By June 28th	June 29th–July 10th	July 11th–August 16th
By June 14th	249	269	289
June 15th–June 27th	____	299	319
June 28th–August 2nd	____	____	399

From London Departing	Los Angeles or Vancouver Returning		
	By June 28th	June 29th–July 10th	July 11th–August 16th
By June 14th	319	339	339
June 15th–June 27th	____	369	389
June 28th–August 2nd	____	____	469

THIRD PART

1c 2c 3a 4b 5d

FOURTH PART

6T 7F 8T 9F 10F 11T 12T
13T 14F

Unit 10

LISTENING 1

Task 3

1c 2d 3b 4b

Task 4

a arranged marriages **b** the two people
c the two people and the go-between
d the two people **e** the parents

Task 6

- Estonia
- 1860s
- a forester; he died of pneumonia

Task 7

c is true

Task 8 (Suggested answer)

My grandmother was the oldest sister of three. At that time, the end of the last century, girls couldn't get married until the older ones had been married and she was rather choosy and couldn't find a husband. The other girls said that they wanted to get married and she was not married. She said: 'All right, I'll accept the next man that comes.' And, of course, that story went round the village and a man came whom she really hated and asked for her hand. She had promised and they got married. They didn't have a very big wedding as far as I have heard, and after six months she was so fed up with the husband that she said she was going to get a divorce. Of course, at that time (it must have been the 1860s), it was very unusual to get a divorce in Estonia, but she got a divorce and married my grandfather, who was a forester. They had two daughters, my mother and her sister. My grandfather was a forester in Alodaguza, which is a really big forest, and he went to the forest and a bear had woken up during hibernation. My grandfather had a real fight with the bear and was injured and apparently fainted and lay in the snow for a long time and got pneumonia and died. When my mother was three, I think.

LISTENING 2

Task 2

1e 2a 3c 4b 5d 6f

Task 3

marry/married/marriage costs offence prolonged subjected happier separated separation different difference

Task 4

aT bF cT dF eT fT gF

Task 5

1a 2a 3b 4b 5b

Task 7

offence obviously bigamy separation nowadays

Task 8

More than thirty per cent of marriages in the United Kingdom end in divorce, the highest rate of any country in Europe. There are also more people who are separated from their husbands and wives than anywhere else. In addition, there are more people in the UK who live together without getting married than in any other country that keeps records of this kind.

SPEAKING

Task 2

b

Task 4

a a short story **b** a local newspaper report
c a gossip column

Exam practice

1c 2b 3a

Unit 11

LISTENING 1

Task 3

Not mentioned: Oxford Circus, Park Lane, Piccadilly Circus, Parliament Square

Task 5

a heavy congestion **b** traffic lights out of order
c broken-down buses **d** roadworks

Task 6

Gerry What's causing all the hold-ups, Amy?
Amy There are just too many cars. And the weather's a problem. More people seem to be on the roads in their cars today because of the rain. I would suggest that anyone listening should come in by train or tube.
Gerry Good idea.

LISTENING 2

Task 1

blackmail assault kidnapping fraud
theft stealing (speeding is also an offence)

Task 3

1a 2b 3a 4a 5b 6b

Task 4

1d 2c 3c 4b 5a 6c

Task 6

/t/ sentenced announced
/d/ discovered accused appeared changed revealed criticised refused named
/ɪd/ arrested pleaded remanded admitted
irregular: stole took hid found

Task 7

Today police arrested a man in connection with the bullion robbery at Salford Security Warehouse, which took place two weeks ago. The man, who has not been named, appeared in court this morning and was charged with robbery. He was remanded in custody for three weeks.

SPEAKING

a suggests a solution
b suggests a cause
c criticises a decision

Exam practice

FIRST PART

	Classwork	Examination
English	D	E
French	A	B
Spanish	B	B
History	B	E
Geography	B	E
Science	A	E
Mathematics	A	D
Art	A	A

SECOND PART

	Departures	
To	**Time**	**Platform**
Bristol	9.20	5
Liverpool	10.45	6
Manchester	9.50	6
Nottingham	9.55	1
Oxford	10.15	2
Sheffield	10.05	4

THIRD PART

1e 2c 3a 4f 5d 6b

FOURTH PART

7c 8a 9d 10c 11a

Unit 12

LISTENING 1

Task 2

1i 2d 3h 4g 5a 6b 7c 8e 9f

Task 3

1b 2c 3c 4a 5a 6c 7a

Task 4

aT bF cT dT eT fF gF hT

Task 5 (Suggested answer)

Basically, a house today doesn't do what busy people need it to do. Take security, for example. A modern house isn't protected. All you have is a simple device like a burglar alarm. Someone opens the front door and the alarm goes off. I've designed a completely new system of burglary prevention. If a burglar breaks into an intelligent house, a heat-sensitive, mobile camera will locate him, the burglar and his picture will appear at a local police station. And the burglar will only have to cough and the police will be able to find him on a computer. And the owner of the house will also carry a little gadget so that he'll be alerted to the danger as well.

Task 6

food and security

Task 8

/ɔː/ bought /əʊ/ though /ʌf/ enough
/ɒf/ cough /uː/ through

Task 9

very soon will be able by the year 2020

LISTENING 2

Task 3

agreed alone attempt ago appear avoid asleep
arrest away aloud/allowed

(underlined words appear in the text, plus greed, tempt, go, sleep, rest, loud)

Task 5

1c 2a 3d 4b 5a 6c 7c

Task 6

Jane: train main plain strain pain
Blake: cake wake sake make take

SPEAKING

Task 4

a no life **b** life **c** life **d** no life

Exam practice

FIRST PART

1c 2c 3c 4d 5c

SECOND PART

6 (for) 11 (against) 9 (for) 7 (against)
10 (for) 8 (against)

THIRD PART

12F 13T 14T 15T 16F 17F

FOURTH PART

LOCAL QUESTIONNAIRE

Local resident? Yes ☑ No ☐

Voted for which party?
Greens ☐ Social Democrats ☑
Conservatives ☐ Socialist Workers ☐

Voting intentions?
Same ☐ Different ☐ Don't know ☑

Most important local issue?
Roads ☐ Old people ☐ Education ☑
Rubbish collection ☐

Children? No ☐ One ☐ More than one ☑

Most Important issue in Education?
More money ☐ New school buildings ☐
Smaller classes ☑

Tapescripts

Starter unit

LISTENING 1

Inspector Mrs Carter?
Mrs Carter Yes?
Inspector Inspector Black of the CID.
Mrs Carter Oh. What can I do for you, inspector?
Inspector Just a couple of questions, Mrs Carter. Are you the owner of this shop?
Mrs Carter Yes, I am.
Inspector And were you here yesterday?
Mrs Carter Yes.
Inspector Can you tell me what time you arrived?
Mrs Carter Yes, but why do you want to know?
Inspector Just a routine enquiry, Mrs Carter. What time did you arrive?
Mrs Carter About 9.30.
Inspector And what time did you leave?
Mrs Carter I stayed until about midday.
Inspector I see. So you weren't here in the afternoon?
Mrs Carter No. What is all this about?
Inspector Was anybody here?
Mrs Carter Inspector, you really must tell me why you're asking all these questions.
Inspector There was a robbery at Milton's Bank yesterday afternoon. The people responsible left the bank … . and disappeared.
Mrs Carter Milton's Bank? Where's that?
Inspector Well, it's in Cross Street. But the back door faces onto the piece of land which is directly behind your shop.
Mrs Carter Really? I didn't know that.
Inspector Was anybody in the shop yesterday afternoon?
Mrs Carter Yes. My shop manager.
Inspector What's his name?
Mrs Carter It isn't a man, it's a woman.
Inspector Sorry. What's her name?
Mrs Carter Catherine Parker.
Inspector I see. Is she coming to the shop today?
Mrs Carter No.
Inspector Why not?
Mrs Carter She doesn't work here on Fridays.
Inspector Fine. Could you let me have her address and telephone number, please?
Mrs Carter Well, I could, but there's no point in contacting her there.
Inspector Why not?
Mrs Carter She went on holiday this morning.
Inspector I see. Where did she go?
Mrs Carter I'm not sure. Trinidad, I think.

LISTENING 2

On July 17th, 1969, Apollo 11 left Cape Kennedy, near Houston in Texas, on a voyage to the moon. Aboard the spacecraft were three American astronauts, Neil Armstrong, Buzz Aldrin and Michael Collins.

The journey lasted for four days. Finally, Apollo went into orbit around the moon. Collins remained in the spacecraft, and the other two descended to the moon's surface in a smaller craft, the lunar module. After a moment of drama, when the two astronauts narrowly avoided landing in a crater, the lunar module finally reached its destination.

So, on July 21st, Armstrong became the first person to set foot on the moon. His first words, as he stood on the lunar surface, were these: 'That's one small step for a man, one giant leap for mankind.'

Armstrong and Aldrin collected samples of dust and rock and took photographs before returning to Apollo for the return journey to Earth.

Unit 1

LISTENING 1

Monica Sometimes it's quite difficult to meet English people and to practise the language … so well the way I practise my English is watching TV most of the time or sometimes I'm just … I'm in the street walking and I just stop people you know in the street plain blond English face looking you know looking face and I just say um I'm sorry er what time is it please you know and then they start saying the time and or maybe you know you appear a bit lost in the street and English people are very helpful and they come to you and they say and can I help you any … anyhow oh yes please! you know I'm really lost and I don't know where this place is and that way you just start a conversation you know it's just a good way of practise … practising the language.
Ken Isn't it a little bit dangerous stopping people in the street like that?
Monica Not really. I wouldn't say so because if you do that in the middle of the day and in a very crowded place which is London really London is a very crowded town I don't see the danger of it you know you're surrounded by people you know daylight and I've got a good pair of legs to run away anyway …
Ken Tell me something else … which of the language skills do you find most difficult?
Monica The most difficult is the pronunciation … I'm still practising it actually see people say I beg your pardon I don't understand what you're saying it's a bit frustrating. I think especially for Latin countries … um … our languages are just so different, the pronunciation and sometimes the grammar especially talking about English grammar. I find it so illogical, it's unreal, there's no logic to it … all these irregular things about it you know
Ken What about listening and speaking and things like that?
Monica Well, I've got no difficulties for speaking because I'm very chatty person and to be honest I don't care if I make mistakes. To me the most important thing is to say things, doesn't matter how and then people they can be very helpful if you're making a mistake they actually say oh I hope you don't mind but actually that's not the right way to say things and then they correct you … .
Ken What about reading and writing?
Monica Reading and writing. Right. I … I read quite a lot and actually I read more in English than in Italian now and I've got to start picking up Italian books as well … um I … I read lots of newspapers you know from the gossipy ones to the more intellectual ones and um but writing I do like writing er when I've got time, I always make the effort to keep in touch with friends and I'm quite confident about my writing because I think I studied quite a lot at school and they've given me a very good basis and I'm very confident in my grammar and in my spelling. I'm sure that I can write better than a normal English person with less spelling mistakes and actually it's amazing when some Americans or English people write me back and I can correct their mistakes. Yeah!

LISTENING 2

Interviewer Hello and welcome to *Who's in Town*. Tonight, I'm very pleased to welcome to the studio the star of the new Australian TV series, *The People Next Door*. Ladies and gentlemen, please welcome … Celia Street!
(Applause)
Interviewer Hello, Celia.
Celia Hello, Jason.
Interviewer *The People Next Door* started broadcasting on British TV only about three months ago.
Celia That's right, but it's already the number one family series.
Interviewer Yes, I was just about to say that myself!
Celia Sorry!
Interviewer That's all right, Celia. What's it like working on the show?
Celia Well, it's pretty hard, actually. I mean … we have to make two episodes a week, so we have to work all day every day, sometimes seven days a week.
Interviewer Yes. Two episodes, that means you have to produce sixty minutes of film every week.
Celia Well, it's about forty-five minutes. There are commercial breaks.
Interviewer Tell us something about your daily routine.
Celia I have to be at the studio by six o'clock in the morning …
Interviewer Six o'clock?!?
Celia Yes, I'm usually in the make-up department by about half past six, and we have our first script meeting at about half past seven, and we're on the set by eight-thirty.
Interviewer And it's like that every day?
Celia Yes. At least five days a week, and sometimes six or seven.
Interviewer And what time do you finish?
Celia It depends what we're filming. Sometimes we're there until eight or nine o'clock at night. And if we're filming night scenes outside, we may be there until after midnight. But if we do that, we usually get a lie-in the next day.

Interviewer What do the people who live in the actual street think about all this filming at night?
Celia What do you mean … the people in the street?
Interviewer The residents of Carey Street, or whatever the real name is.
Celia It isn't a real street.
Interviewer What?
Celia It isn't a real street!
Interviewer Not a real street?
Celia No! I thought everybody knew that!
Interviewer I didn't! I thought it was a real street!
Celia No … it's a studio set! It's in the car-park behind the TV studio!
Interviewer It must be enormous!
Celia What?
Interviewer The car-park.
Celia Why?
Interviewer There are so many houses in the street … the car-park must be enormous.
Celia Oh, I see. No, most of the houses are only facades.
Interviewer You're joking!
Celia No, I'm not. They're made of plastic.
Interviewer Really? That's amazing! well … you learn something new every day. Celia … you said you have to be in the studio at six o'clock in the morning.
Celia Yes, that's right.
Interviewer What time do you get up?
Celia About five o'clock.
Interviewer Five o'clock … don't you find it difficult getting up so early in the morning?
Celia Yes … impossible! I get an alarm call at a quarter to five, and then the studio car arrives at about a quarter to six.
Interviewer Do you go out in the evening? Do you have any kind of social life?
Celia Not at the moment, no. We spend a bit of time together when we finish filming. You know the kind of thing, we go off to an Italian restaurant, something like that. We all get on with each other very well.
Interviewer Just in case there's anyone listening who hasn't seen *The People Next Door*, tell us something about the character you play.
Celia Well, I play an English girl called Elizabeth who has just arrived in the neighbourhood. Her family has emigrated from England and everything is very different. She spends most of her time getting things wrong because she doesn't understand what people are saying, or she doesn't understand the money. She goes to the local high school, which is very different from the school she went to in England.
Interviewer Is it similar to what happened to you when you went to Australia?
Celia Not really, no.
Interviewer Your family actually live in Sydney, don't they?
Celia Not exactly. My brother Les lives in Sydney. He moved there a couple of years ago because he was playing in a band with a couple of Australians. I went out to see him last summer, saw the job advertised and applied for it. The rest of our family still live in England.
Interviewer Do you like living in Australia?
Celia Well, I like working in Sydney. I never have time to do anything except work. I don't get the chance to find out what Australia is really like.
Interviewer What do you do on days when you're not filming?
Celia I sleep!

Exam practice: paper 4

FIRST PART

This is the Odeon Cinema information line. Here are details of the films that we are showing at the cinema from next Monday.

In Cinema One, from Monday to Thursday, we're showing *Rainman*, with Dustin Hoffmann and Tom Cruise, and this film will transfer to Cinema Four from Friday to Sunday, all performances except late-night Friday and Saturday.

Cinema Two is showing *Baghdad Cafe*, a film directed by Percy Adlon, all performances except Friday and Saturday late-night.

In Cinema Three, we have a season of John Ford Westerns, with a different film every night, except Friday and Saturday late-night when you can see *Baghdad Cafe* on this screen. Look in the local papers for details of which John Ford film will be showing on any particular night.

The Peter Greenaway season continues in Cinema Four with performances of *Drowning by Numbers* from Monday to Thursday and late-night Friday and Saturday. This film will also be shown in Cinema One from Friday to Sunday, except late-night.

This week in Cinema Five, we start a new season of comedy classics with the Billy Wilder film *Some Like It Hot*, starring Marilyn Monroe, Tony Curtis and Jack Lemmon. This film is also showing in Cinema One, late-night Friday and Saturday.

Other late-night films on Friday and Saturday are as follows: Cinema Two is showing *Rainman* and Cinema Five one of the John Ford Westerns. We hope that this has cleared up any confusion about the films you can see at your local Odeon.

SECOND PART

A Excuse me, sir?
B Yes?
A Do you mind answering a few questions?
B What about?
A It's a public transport survey.
B Oh, all right.
A Now … first question … do you use public transport every day?
B No … well, do you mean seven days a week?
A No, weekdays … Monday to Friday.
B Yes, I do.
A And weekends?
B It depends.
A Would you say you used it regularly, occasionally or rarely?
B Not very much at all really, only about once a month. I usually spend the weekends away.
A OK. And why do you use public transport during the week?
B Monday to Friday?
A Yes.
B To go to work.
A Where do you work?
B Hanbury's. It's a clothes shop.
A Where's that?
B Cross Street.
A OK … central area. Do you make the journey to work at this time every day?
B Yes … between eight and nine.
A Can you be more precise?
B Well … usually between 8.30 and 8.45.
A And what time do you arrive at work?
B About half an hour later.
A What about your return journey?
B About 5.15.
A 5.15. Is that when you leave work or arrive home?
B I leave at 5.15. I arrive home about six. I don't know why but it takes longer in the evening.
A Arriving home at six o'clock …
B Except Thursdays. I work late on a Thursday.
A Do you always take the same route?
B Yes. Number 15 bus. It's the only one that goes anywhere near Cross Street.
A Have you got a season ticket?
B No, I haven't.
A Why not? Are they too expensive?
B They may be too expensive … I don't know. I haven't got one because I'm trying to get another job so I expect I'll be moving in the not too distant future.
A OK, sir. Thanks for your help.
B Pleasure.

THIRD PART

People often ask me to explain the behaviour of their pets. Many of them talk about their cats and dogs as if they were talking about other people. Some people insist that their animals think and behave exactly like human beings. 'He knows exactly what I'm thinking about' and 'You could see that he knew he'd done something wrong' are two examples that crop up very often in conversations with pet-owners.

Sadly, I have to inform these people that almost without exception, the behaviour of their pets bears no resemblance at all to human behaviour. Let's look at some of the more obvious examples.

Dogs wag their tails when their owners come home from work. It looks as if they're pleased to see their human companions. This is not true. They're hungry. They associate the arrival of a human with the arrival of food. If you don't believe me, try this experiment: for a week, feed your dog when you leave home, not when you arrive. Very quickly, the dog will begin to wag its tail when it sees you getting ready to leave, rather than when you arrive.

The other great mistake that owners make about dogs in particular is to think that animals have any sense of guilt. They have no such sense. If an owner finds a dog eating a piece of steak that the owner was about to eat, there is predictable and very basic behaviour on both sides. The owner screams at the dog and the dog hides under the nearest table. The owner screams because he or she is angry. The dog hides because it feels afraid, *not* because it feels guilty. If the dog stays away from the steak next time (which can't be guaranteed because most dogs are extremely stupid), the reason is fear of punishment, not that the dog feels guilty.

And what about cats? Ah ... cats, now they really *are* intelligent, or so most people seem to think. They don't wag their tails and make fools of themselves like dogs. They're much too intelligent for that. Sorry ... once again, I have to inform people that there is no obvious difference in intelligence between cats and dogs. The behaviour of domestic cats and dogs simply resembles the behaviour of their relatives in the wild. Dogs are descended from wolves, who spend a lot of time in packs and exhibit the social habits of packs, making a lot of noise and playing a lot. The relatives of cats in the wild, particularly tigers, spend much more time alone, particularly when hunting. As a result, they have developed more solitary tendencies. And cats are particularly keen on sleeping in warm places, which is why they prefer sleeping on people rather than floors.

FOURTH PART

There are in existence computers that know how to predict the weather better than any farmer, that can tell you if a seat is available on an aeroplane leaving an airport 10,000 kilometres away and can do mathematical problems of incredible complexity. A human mathematician would take months to solve a problem which some computers could probably solve in less than a millionth of a second. Computers like this seem to be cleverer than people, but they aren't really. Every computer needs a person to tell it what to do.

In fact, computers are just machines that do three things: they store information, they retrieve information and they manipulate information, or data. This data can be numbers, if the computer is being used as a sophisticated calculator, or words, if the computer is being used as a word processor, which is like a sophisticated typewriter and filing system.

There are four basic units in a computer, an input unit, a memory, a central processing unit and an output unit.

The input unit is usually a keyboard and by using the keyboard like an ordinary typewriter, data is stored inside the memory. Although it looks like an ordinary typewriter, a computer keyboard does much more than simply type words. It obeys commands ... it stores and retrieves information at the touch of a button, if you know the right codes to operate it.

The data that is put into the computer via the keyboard is stored in a part of the memory unit called the RAM, which stands for 'Random Access Memory'. There is another part of the memory which is called ROM and this stands for 'Read Only Memory'. Information which is stored here consists of instructions and other constant data that cannot be changed. The data that you retrieve and manipulate is stored in the RAM.

The keyboard, the RAM and the ROM are all connected to the central processing unit and this unit sends the results of your work to the output unit, which can be a printer or a screen which looks like a television set and is called a Visual Display Unit, or VDU.

To make it all work, a computer needs a program which tells it what to do. Without a program, a computer isn't really very clever at all.

Unit 2

● LISTENING 1

(Phone ringing)

Archer Extension 231.
Sharp Mr Archer?
Archer Yes?
Sharp It's Peter Sharp.
Archer Er ...
Sharp About the loan. I spoke to you yesterday.
Archer Oh yes, Mr Sharp. Sorry.
Sharp That's all right.
Archer Well, I've got the form in front of me. Shall I send it to you, or can you give me the details over the phone?
Sharp I can tell you now, if you like.
Archer Fine. Your full name is ...
Sharp Peter Victor Sharp.
Archer And your address?
Sharp 27 Petley Lane.
Archer Where's that?
Sharp In Chelsea.
Archer What do you do, Mr Sharp?
Sharp I'm a production controller at a computer assembly plant.
Archer And how much do you earn?
Sharp About £600 a month, after tax.
Archer How long have you been working at the plant, Mr Sharp?
Sharp A week.
Archer Hm. Is it a permanent position?
Sharp I'm on a month's trial. Dependent on that, I may get a permanent job.
Archer I see. Are you married?
Sharp Yes.
Archer Does your wife work?
Sharp Yes, she works in a shop.
Archer What kind of shop?
Sharp Well, at the moment, she's working in a supermarket.
Archer I see. Have you got any children?
Sharp No.
Archer What kind of place do you live in?
Sharp A house.
Archer Do you live in the whole house?
Sharp No. We live in a flat on the top floor.
Archer OK ... is it yours?
Sharp How do you mean?
Archer Do you rent it or are you buying it?
Sharp I rent it.
Archer Right. And one final question, Mr Sharp. Do you smoke?
Sharp Do I what?
Archer Smoke. Are you a smoker?
Sharp Yes, but is that important?
Archer Well, the loans department like to know these things. Anyway, thanks for the information. I'll be in touch as soon as we make our decision. Bye for now.
Sharp Goodbye.

● LISTENING 2

Reporter I'm standing right in the middle of the ground floor of the new Blandsmere Shopping Centre in Croydon, about fifteen miles from the centre of London. It's a huge, square indoor complex, with an extraordinary variety of shops and a large open-plan restaurant here in the middle.

Right in front of me, I can see Tessman's Supermarket, the biggest one I've ever seen. That takes up the whole of the north side of the square. On my left, on the west side of the square, there are three shops ... a videomarket, a computer shop and a furniture store. On my right, on the east side, are a series of smaller shops ... I can see a greetings card shop, next to that a record store ... and more shops selling toys, gifts and flowers.

Behind me is the main entrance to the complex, on the south side, directly opposite the big Tessmanns Supermarket. There's a large shop on each side of the main entrance. On the left of the entrance as I look at it is Marstons Shoes, and on the right, a shop called the Wholefood Delicatessen.

And here right at the centre is a restaurant with about thirty tables set in a circle around a circular bar. The kitchen is downstairs in the basement. The effect is very continental, with people sitting around drinking coffee or enjoying snacks or meals.

Although the Shopping Centre is completely enclosed, you get the feeling that you're out in the open air because the whole thing is encased in a glass dome roof.

What makes the complex quite unusual is the variety of facilities and attractions that you can find here. On the upper floor, there's a large sports complex above the supermarket on the north side, and a swimming pool and sauna on the south side. On the east side is a line of cosmopolitan restaurants and cafes, where you can try Indian, Chinese and many other styles of food.

Opposite that, there's a motel ... the first motel ever to be built in a British shopping complex.

I recommend that you visit the Blandsmere Centre at the first opportunity.

Unit 3

● LISTENING 1

Interviewer John, you like horror films, don't you?
John Yes, I do.
Interviewer When was the first horror film made?
John The first horror film was actually made in 1898.
Interviewer Really?
John Can you believe that? And in fact they were made all through the silent era ... er ... but in fact my favourite kinds of horror films were the ones that were made in the 1940s and 1950s, what we call B-movie horror films and also the Hammer horror films ...
Interviewer Hammer horror films?
John Yes.
Interviewer What were they?
John Well, they were films that were made in the 1950s and early 1960s. I think the first one was made in 1958. It was Dracula, which ...er ... had an actor called Christopher Lee in it.

Interviewer Oh. Not Bela Lugosi ...?

John No. Now Bela Lugosi was a silent film actor. He made a very, very good film called Dracula I think in the 1920s. No, the Hammer Horror films had all the same actors in, there was Christopher Lee and Peter Cushing and another favourite actor of mine was Vincent Price. He worked with a director called Roger Corman.

Interviewer Roger Corman is an American. Is that right?

John That's right and he specialised in low-budget horror films and he actually gave Jack Nicholson his first break in the movies.

Interviewer Really?

John Yes.

Interviewer What was the horror film that Jack Nicholson was in?

John Well, he appeared in two. He appeared in The Raven ... er ... with Vincent Price and Peter Lorre and Boris Karloff and he also appeared in the original movie version of The Little Shop Of Horrors, which people now know is a musical.

Interviewer Yes. What is it that fascinates you about horror films, then?

John Well, I enjoy the sensation of being afraid. I like watching horror films by myself in a dark room and I just enjoy the sensation. I also am very interested in special effects and I think if you want to see good special effects, you have to watch a horror movie or ... um ... a science fiction movie.

Interviewer Mm. The sort of horror films that I can remember seeing always involve a big, old, dark kind of Gothic house. Why do they always use houses like that?

John I think that all started in the novels of Edgar Allan Poe, er, some terrific horror stories there, short stories and novels. In fact, The Raven, the Roger Corman film, was an Edgar Allan Poe novel. They all use this house on a hill in a storm or in a forest or somewhere out of the way where you're isolated. I think that's why Psycho is so memorable as well because it's an isolated place and the image of the house on the hill. People can imagine themselves being there and being in that situation. They never have telephones and the electricity never works and there's always a cellar. It's the darkness in all of us.

LISTENING 2

1 You feed your cat every day, but does he get all the nutrition he needs? New **Kattomilk** is a special preparation that will do just that. It's a milk drink that's rich in vitamins. Try it and see what he thinks. When he's tried Kattomilk, he'll never want to drink ordinary milk again.

2 No one likes to come home and find that their house has been ransacked. It's even worse when you know they got in because your doors and windows weren't securely locked. Do the sensible thing ... fit **Securex** locks to all your doors and windows. Securex locks protect your house from unwelcome visitors. So ... fit Securex ... before it's too late!

3 We offered **Seafresh** Washing Powder to twenty-five housewives in the Luton area, completely free for three weeks. At the end of the test period, all twenty-five said they definitely preferred Seafresh to their old washing powder. Seafresh clean is deep down clean. Seafresh ... try it yourself and see. It's special.

4 New **Carcover** Insurance gives you the insurance you need if you're driving in today's high-speed world.
We guarantee that we can get you back on the road faster than any other insurance company. And back on the road means back in business. Fast. Easy. No problem with Carcover. Get Carcover. Get peace of mind. Call Carcover first.

5 Sally Richards talks about the **Sunday Post**: 'I love it ... it's got everything I could possibly want in a Sunday newspaper. I'd rather read the Sunday Post than anything else. Yes ... you could say I prefer the Sunday Post!' Sally Richards reads the *Sunday Post*. Read it on Sunday and you could win an exciting holiday for two in Madagascar. The *Sunday Post*. Read it.

6 **Bensons's** Sale is now on. Unbeatable value on furniture, carpets, curtains and clothes. Everything at half price in the sale to end all sales. Come to Benson's, the bargain store.

7 When Alison Watson won the Bristol Marathon, she was wearing **Bantams**. Bantam Runners ... the running shoe that nine out of ten winners prefer. Buy now and take advantage of the Bantam Special Offer ... £5 off the recommended price if you buy two pairs.

Exam practice: paper 4

FIRST PART

If you're the kind of person who likes to sit at a desk all day and then spend the next two hours behind the wheel of a car listening to Barry Manilow, the Kingsland Fitness Centre is not for you. But if you need to work out after work, the Kingsland is the place to go.

We're sure you'll love the Kingsland. The studios are light and airy and we offer a variety of classes, including general fitness and stamina programmes. Or, if you prefer, you can spend the evening in our sauna and steam room suite followed by a nutritious snack in our vegetarian restaurant. But we think the place you will really love is the gymnasium, full of all the latest in exercise technology. And of course there's the swimming pool, with freshly-made juices available at the poolside bar.

The feature that really makes the Kingsland special is the personal training programme. We can prepare for you a training programme that is just for you, what you need to do but also what you like to do. Tell us the kind of activities that you prefer, and we'll turn them into a fitness programme that suits you.

Come and have a look at the Kingsland. You'll love it!

SECOND PART

Salesman That's thirteen pounds for the petrol. Here's your change.

Customer Thank you.

Salesman And here are your coupons. Do you collect our coupons?

Customer No. What are they for?

Salesman Free gifts. You collect coupons at any Vulcan Oil Station and then you exchange them for free gifts. This is our catalogue. Have a look.

Customer I don't understand. You said 'free gifts'. It says coupons plus cash here.

Salesman Well, you can choose. You can either collect enough coupons to get the gift for nothing, or if you prefer, you can collect fewer coupons and pay some cash. Take the luggage for example. The two weekend cases ... 500 coupons or 200 coupons plus £30 in cash.

Customer And the camera is 75 coupons?

Salesman No, 750. 750 coupons, or 500 and £25 in cash.

Customer That's expensive.

Salesman No, it's a quality camera. Anyway, you don't need to spend any money at all. Keep buying Vulcan petrol and you get them free. And some of them are not expensive at all. Look at this nice CD rack ...

Customer What?

Salesman A CD rack. It's a place to stack your Compact Discs.

Customer I haven't got any Compact Discs.

Salesman Well, you never know ... you may one day. Anyway, it's only 100 coupons.

Customer It doesn't say anything about coupons and cash.

Salesman No, we don't accept cash for the CD rack, or for the keyring. That's only ten coupons, by the way.

Customer I don't like the look of that key-ring ... it's advertising Vulcan Oil.

Salesman What about the emergency light? Very smart, very useful ... 200 coupons, or 100 coupons and £10.

Customer How many coupons for this calculator?

Salesman Ah ... that's not a calculator, it's an electronic address book. Very nice.

Customer I don't like it. It's ugly.

Salesman Well, it's very useful and only 600 coupons. Or 300 coupons and £30.

Customer I like this ... it's a clock radio, isn't it?

Salesman Alarm-clock radio, yes. Very good value. 500 coupons, or 400 coupons and £10.

Customer Well, I'll start saving for one of those. It looks very nice indeed.

THIRD PART

The agent for the anonymous Japanese buyer of Van Gogh's Portrait of Doctor Gachet announced at the end of the auction that he had been instructed to buy the painting 'at any price'. With people bidding for famous paintings with these instructions in mind, it's no wonder that the prices of works of art by famous painters are reaching such ridiculous levels.

The Portrait of Doctor Gachet is not a masterpiece. It was painted by Van Gogh towards the end of his life and is generally regarded as one of his average works. And yet someone paid more than eighty million dollars for it. Why? Because it was available. No other reason.

Paintings by the great masters, Van Gogh, Picasso, and the French Impressionists particularly, are now in such heavy demand that there are almost none left in private collections, although in Picasso's case, this is partly because his paintings have the rare distinction of being stolen more often than those of other great artists.

But an art collector with a Van Gogh or a Monet in his or her attic will have to love that painting a great deal to turn down an offer of more than fifty million dollars. And there is still, it seems, more money to spend in this way. Art galleries in California are under instructions to spend whatever is necessary to make that state's art collection more valuable than the collections on the East Coast of the USA in New York and Boston. It would be impossible to make the West Coast collections more valuable. On the other hand, there is no doubt that the Californian collection will soon be more expensive.

FOURTH PART

Interviewer Ok, that brings to an end our trio of golden hits from the sixties, and now we're going to hear what our trio of kids from the nineties think about them. Rob, you first.

Rob Well, I didn't like the second one at all …

Interviewer The Rolling Stones record …

Rob Yes, I didn't like the tune and I didn't like the words. I didn't really understand what it was about.

Interviewer Well, it's called 'Sympathy for the Devil'.

Rob Hm. Well, I didn't like it at all.

Anna I thought it was terrific.

Interviewer Did you, Anna?

Anna Yes.

Interviewer Did you understand what it was about?

Anna Well, not really, but I liked it.

Interviewer What about you, Steve?

Steve I thought it was awful. I've heard that track before and I didn't like it at all. I loved that third song, though. Who was that by?

Interviewer The Who.

Steve Who?

Interviewer The Who. That's the name of the group.

Steve Oh right, The Who. Well, the song is terrific.

Interviewer Anybody know what it's called?

Anna Isn't it called 'Pinball'?

Interviewer Almost. It's called 'Pinball Wizard'. It's from a rock opera called *Tommy*. Did you like it, Anna?

Anna Yes. Loved it.

Interviewer Rob?

Rob I didn't like it at all.

Interviewer What did you think of the first song?

Rob Well that was the Beatles, wasn't it?

Interviewer Yes.

Rob And the song was 'Penny Lane'.

Interviewer Correct.

Rob Well, actually I like the Beatles very much …

Interviewer Great!

Rob … But I can't stand that song.

Interviewer Oh.

Anna I didn't like it, either. I always thought Penny Lane was the name of a girl, but I don't think it is, is it?

Steve No. It's the name of a street in Liverpool. I think 'Penny Lane' is a great song myself.

Interviewer Good. Well, that's the end of our discussion about hits from the sixties. Tune in next week and we'll be playing songs by Bob Dylan, Elvis Presley and Eric Clapton's old band, Cream.

Unit 4

● LISTENING 1

Here is the weather forecast for Great Britain and Northern Ireland for tomorrow, Tuesday the fourth of August. First of all, the forecast for six o'clock in the morning.

In Northern Ireland and Scotland, it will be cloudy with occasional showers. Winds will be light and from the north east and there will be mist in sheltered areas. Temperatures will be around six Celsius.

In Wales and Northern England, it will be cloudy with more showers and occasional bright intervals. Winds will be from the south west and temperatures will be higher than the seasonal average at around ten to twelve Celsius.

In South West and Central England, the morning will start wet and windy and it will be cool but not as cool as other parts of the country. The South East and East Anglia will start bright with sunny intervals, although there will be fog patches in coastal areas. Temperatures in the south will be around twelve Celsius.

And now the forecast for midday:

By midday tomorrow, the picture will be quite different. Northern Ireland and Scotland will be mainly sunny with temperatures of twelve degrees Celsius, although a strong east wind will make it seem cooler. Wales and Northern England will experience much heavier rain and cooler temperatures than the rest of the country, with much stronger winds from the south east.

In South West and Central England, the wet and windy start will give way to much warmer weather due to a warm breeze coming from the south east, with occasional bright spells and sunshine. In the South East and East Anglia, expect occasional thunderstorms and heavy rain. Temperatures in this area will be about average.

All in all, a pretty normal day for the weather.

● LISTENING 2

Interviewer Today we're focusing on the problem of noise, noise at home and noise at work. Medical experts agree that there are definite links between noise and stress levels … the noisier the environment, the more stress you are likely to experience. And it's even worse when a person is forced to live and work in noisy environments. This seems to have been the problem for Ann Dickinson.

Ann … the first place I lived in when I moved here was really lousy. It was on a main road … I was used to living out in the country. There were lorries passing by the front door all day and all night. Then the local council put a ban on trucks using that road during the night, so things got marginally better and I got a bit more sleep. But then I decided to move and things got much worse …

Interviewer Ann moved from her house on the main road to a block of flats. It was next to a park, so it should have been quieter, but it wasn't.

Ann … the problem in the next place was the neighbours … the people directly upstairs from me. They played music all night long and got very shirty when I asked them to stop. The police used to come round two or three times a week, but they only stopped for a few minutes and then set off again even louder. I mean … the problem for me was that there was no break. It was noisy where I lived and noisy where I worked.

Interviewer Ann was working in a laundry, the only job that she could find when she left school and decided at the same time to move away from her home town. Her doctor advised her to look for a job in a quieter environment.

Ann … it was all very well telling me to get a quieter job. If you've got qualifications,you can do what you like. If you're not qualified, you've got to take what you can get. Anyway, I did what the doctor told me … I left the laundry and went to work in a factory. I was worse off, but it was quieter.

Interviewer Ann was lucky enough to move to a really modern factory where the work involved assembling car stereos. The change she experienced was remarkable.

Ann … I used to feel a pain in my back and my shoulders while I was walking to the laundry. I didn't realise it was stress. After a week at the factory, I really perked up. I suddenly noticed that the pain had gone. Then I started feeling more energetic and I didn't feel so tired at the end of the day. I mean … the difference was quite incredible.

Interviewer There was still the problem of the noisy neighbours. Fortunately for Ann, a change was about to take place.

Ann They moved out. It's much quieter now. The new people in the flat upstairs make less noise than I do! They're so quiet, I think they must tiptoe everywhere. When I think about the way things were, the contrast is incredible. There's really no comparison.

Unit 5

● LISTENING 1

Hello. You have dialled the number of the International Jobline, the telephone employment service. Today we have a selection of positions for linguists, translators and interpreters.

The first job is based in Paris, working for an international company specialising in high-fashion clothing. The managing director of the company needs a personal secretary who is fluent in at least two of the following languages: German, Italian, Greek and Spanish, as well as speaking good French and English. Applicants should have some experience of working in the clothing industry. The starting salary for the successful applicant will be 12,000 francs per month. Interviews will take place in Paris, London and Rome during April.

The second job we are offering today is based at the European Commission building in Brussels. It's for an interpreter who can speak English, French and Dutch and who has experience of simultaneous translation work. The starting salary is 60,000 Belgian francs per month. All reasonable removal expenses will be paid and assistance will be given in finding accommodation in Brussels.

The third position we are advertising is for a translator. A publishing house based in Athens is looking for someone who can translate American and English scientific books into Greek and Italian. The work is offered on a freelance basis, although it will be more or less full-time for the first six months. There is no regular salary offered for this position. The successful applicant will be paid a fee for each book that he or she translates. Preference will be given to applicants who are already living in Greece, or who are able to move to Greece if offered the job.

● LISTENING 2

Ken Tony, where did you go to school?

Tony I went to school in Dublin at a school called St Condlett's College. Condlett was an ancient Irish saint.

Ken Now what age did you start at that school?

Tony Er ... when I was twelve and I was there until I finished at seventeen or eighteen.

Ken And what about before that?

Tony Before that er I had been at a primary school um what in Ireland in those days was called a national school that is to say you didn't actually pay for it so I had the experience of going from a very posh infant school which was run by nuns then to this er national school where the social context was completely different from what I'd come from and then to this um rather posh secondary school ... I had the whole range of social experience in education in Ireland.

Ken Is the system of education the same as it is in Britain?

Tony Broadly speaking, yes, there are many similarities but there are some important differences. One of the key differences is that education in Ireland has been, and some people would say even still is, dominated by the church and by religious people who were teachers ... um ... there are of course disadvantages to this but there are many advantages also. The ... er ... academic standards and achievements tend to be very high and ... um ... they succeed in motivating students to work hard.

Ken And would you call it a comprehensive system, as we call it in Britain?

Tony No, absolutely not a comprehensive system. I mean,that's where it is completely different. In addition to being dominated by the church until 1966, I think, virtually all education in Ireland was private, you had to pay for it. That's why I mentioned this national school I went to. There you didn't pay but everybody only had compulsory and state provided education to the age of twelve. That did change in '66 but the generation that I come from was very much brought up ... er ... on the idea that you had to pay for education and parents would save in order to provide children with a secondary school opportunity. In that respect, it's very like certain countries in Europe where parents work hard specially to provide education for their children so ... no, it's not at all a comprehensive system. Not at all.

Ken So before 1966 ... er ... people who couldn't afford to send their children to secondary school—what happened to those children?

Tony Well, they left school at twelve. Precisely because education was difficult to get and expensive, very high value was placed on it. For Irish people, it's very important and they are very prepared to make sacrifices in order to get education. Um ... I sometimes find the contrast in this country very striking where people seem to think that somehow education is a right that they just have and can confidently expect.

Exam practice: paper 4

FIRST PART

Her maiden name was Agatha Miller and she was born in Torquay. Her American father was an aficionado of amateur dramatics and her mother claimed to be a mind-reader. Her brother was famous for his practical jokes and her sister loved disguises.

In 1914, Agatha married an air force pilot called Archie Christie and this marriage lasted for twenty years. During the First World War, she worked as a dispenser in a pharmacy and learned a lot about poisons. This information was to come in very useful in her many murder mystery stories.

She began her writing career, however, with a series of romantic novels, written under the pseudonym of Mary Westmacott. However, after reading a novel called *The Mystery of the Yellow Room,* she turned her attention to mystery writing. The detective in *The Yellow Room* was an amusing Frenchman named Joseph Rouletabille and Agatha decided to borrow this idea. Possibly because of the large number of Belgian refugees in Torquay at the time, her detective was a French-speaker from Brussels called Hercule Poirot.

Her other famous crime-solving character was an elderly English lady called Miss Marple, who was always able to solve crimes faster than any professional detective.

In 1990, the centenary of her birth, sales of her books in English had reached one billion. She has been translated into forty-four different languages, and these foreign-language editions have sold another billion copies.

Some people are unimpressed by her style and less than enthusiastic about her books, but everyone agrees about her skill as a story-teller. You simply cannot put one of her books down until you have discovered who did it, who committed the crime.

SECOND PART

There are probably more insects in five square kilometres of Brazilian rainforest than there are people in the world. Worldwide, the number is too huge to begin to estimate. And some of the smallest and most ordinary of our insect neighbours have skills and abilities that make human achievement seem very ordinary indeed.

Take the common flea, for example. Everyone knows that fleas jump in the air. What is not such common knowledge is how high they jump. When a flea jumps, it is the equivalent of a human jumping to the top of the Eiffel Tower in Paris. Not once, but 30,000 times, without stopping or getting tired. And the flea's acceleration when jumping is the equivalent of twenty times the rate of a moon rocket leaving Earth's atmosphere.

One of the least pleasant insects, the tick, is also one of the wonders of nature. Ticks, which survive on a diet of the blood of other creatures, including humans, are nature's most successful survivors. They can survive starvation for up to five years, and have been known to live for up to twenty-five.

When it comes to communcation, insects often make humans seem very inarticulate indeed. The honey bee, for example, is extremely skilful at communicating to other honey bees the location of the nectar which is vital to the production of their honey.

When a honey bee finds a new source of the all-important nectar, it returns to the hive to give its colleagues detailed information about the location and quality of the essential material. It performs an elaborate figure-of-eight dance, which indicates to the other honey-bees exactly how far from the hive the nectar is. It also indicates the quality of the nectar by dancing vigorously if the nectar is good and slowly if the nectar is not so good. And by following the direction of the honey-bee's body during this information session, the other bees know exactly the direction they must fly in order to locate the source of the nectar.

THIRD PART

Interviewer Sit down, Mr Truelove.

Truelove Thank you.

Interviewer Can I just check your name and address again?

Truelove Yes. Michael John Truelove.

Interviewer How do you spell that?

Truelove T-R-U-E-L-O-V-E.

Interviewer And your address?

Truelove 26 Rudland Square, Reading.

Interviewer Rutland Square?

Truelove No, Rudland. R-U-D-L-A-N-D.

Interviewer Rudland Square. And Reading is spelt like 'reading', isn't it?

Truelove Yes. R-E-A-D-I-N-G.

Interviewer Right. Now, in front of you is the list of requirements for the job. Have you read it?

Truelove Yes.

Interviewer So, let's go through it. Have you got any A-levels?

Truelove Yes, three.

Interviewer What subjects?

Truelove English, German and Russian.

Interviewer And have you got a degree?

Truelove Yes. In Russian and German.

Interviewer I see. Where did you do that?

Truelove Brunel University.

Interviewer How do you spell 'Brunel'?

Truelove B-R-U-N-E-L.

Interviewer OK. Now, as you know, we need people who are multilingual.

Truelove Well, I'm certainly that.

Interviewer Which languages do you speak?

Truelove Russian, German, French and Swedish.

Interviewer Swedish?

Truelove I've got a Swedish mother.

Interviewer I see. What's your degree of fluency in these languages?

Truelove I'm fluent in Russian and German, about average in French and I'm afraid my Swedish is a bit rusty.

Interviewer We'll put down 'elementary', shall we?

Truelove That seems reasonable.

Interviewer Now, what about business qualifications. Have you got any?

Truelove No.

Interviewer No?

Truelove I'm studying Business Administration at night school at the moment.

Interviewer But you haven't got your MBA.

Truelove What's an MBA?

Interviewer Master of Business Administration.

Truelove No, I'm not studying for that.

Interviewer What about Word Processing? Can you do that?

Truelove I'm afraid I haven't tried.

Interviewer Not to worry. One final thing ... can you drive?

Truelove No.
Interviewer OK. Well … thank you for coming in. We'll be in touch.
Truelove Thank you.

FOURTH PART

According to the *Guinness Book of Records,* the two most travelled people in the world are Parke Thompson of Ohio in the USA and Giorgio Ricatto of Turin, Italy. Both of them have been to all 170 sovereign countries in the world and sixty-two of the sixty-three non-sovereign territories.

A number of people claim to have walked round the world. This is literally impossible, of course, because of the oceans, but nevertheless, some of the achievements are very impressive. David Kunst, for example, an American from Minnesota, can claim to be the first man to have walked around the world. he left home on 20th June 1970 and returned to the USA in October 1974. He walked through America, Europe, Asia and Australia. An Argentinian, Tomas Carlos Pereira, spent ten years, from 1968 to 1978, walking 48,000 kilometres around five continents. Even more incredibly, a Canadian named Rick Hansen travelled more than 40,000 kilometres and visited thirty-four countries in a wheelchair. His journey took him two years.

The *Guinness Book of Records* lists many other similar feats of endurance. An Englishman from Rainham in Kent, George Meegan, walked more than 30,000 kilometres from the southern tip of South America to Northern Alaska between January 1977 and September 1983. Another Englishman, John Lees from Brighton, holds the record for the fastest walk across the United States. He walked from Los Angeles to New York in fifty-three days, twelve hours and fifteen minutes, at an average speed of 86.49 kilometres per day.

Unit 6

● LISTENING 1

Ken Tell me about your family.
Nellie I was born after my father died … six weeks and I had two brothers killed in the First World War … leaving my mother with seven children to look after.
Ken What do you know about your father?
Nellie My father was a law writer for a solicitor. He was a marvellous writer.
Ken Do you know anything about his family, your father's family?
Nellie I slightly remember my father … having two sisters who I think came to live with us when I was born for a few years to help look after us.
Ken Tell me something about your mother.
Nellie My mother was in service when she was young.
Ken What exactly does that mean?
Nellie She … she worked for a rich family.
Ken And where did you all live?
Nellie We lived at number nine Rochester Avenue, in Salford, Lancashire.
Ken Tell me about the house.
Nellie We had three bedrooms … hall,a parlour, a kitchen, a scullery, a backyard and an outside toilet.
Ken Tell me something about the school that you went to.
Nellie I went to St Ambrose school, church school, where we had to go to church every Friday morning. We weren't allowed in church without a hat and so there was always a fight between my sisters and myself to find a hat.
Ken Tell me something about the way, for example, that houses were heated. What did you do for heating?
Nellie With a coal fire. We used to have the coal … delivered in the street … we … had grids in the street where the coal was put down into the cellar … and it was our job when we came home from school to shovel all this coal into the cellar.
Ken Um … when did you first go to work?
Nellie When I was sixteen, I went to work at the local Tramways department, which is now known as Salford Transport.
Ken And what did you do there?
Nellie I was a clerk in the ticket office.
Ken When did you meet your husband?
Nellie I met my husband at a NALGO dance in 1931.
Ken What does NALGO stand for?
Nellie National and Local Government Officers.
Ken OK … and tell me something about him.
Nellie He worked in the Treasurer's Department of the local Town Hall.
Ken How old were you when you got married?
Nellie I was twenty-four when I got married, in June 1935.
Ken You went to work at the Tramways. Tell me something about what your brothers and sisters did.
Nellie Elsie worked in Lewis's, a big store in Manchester. Emily worked in a solicitor's office. Arthur was a draughtsman. Herbert was an upholsterer. Amy was a tailoress. John was an engineer. Agnes was in the sewing trade. I hardly remember my two brothers that were killed in the war. And I had a brother and sister who were born and died before I was born. I don't know anything about them.

● LISTENING 2

Quizmaster Hello and welcome once again to the History Quiz, the quiz that concentrates on historical events and personalities. The quiz is in two parts. In the first part, contestants here in the studio have a chance to answer fifteen questions about the past. There is one point for each correct answer. You the listeners can try to answer these questions as well. In the second part, the questions are especially for you listening at home.
First of all, let's meet our three studio contestants.
Shirley My name is Shirley Grant, and I'm a computer programmer from Nottingham.
Michael My name is Michael Rimmer. I'm from St Helens in Lancashire and I teach Earth Science.
Christine My name is Christine Burrows, and I'm an air traffic controller from Newbury in Berkshire.
(Studio applause)
Quizmaster Now, each of you has a button in front of you,which you must press if you think you know the answers. Can we just have a practice, please?
(Buzz, Ring, Hoot)
Quizmaster Now … put your fingers on your buttons and get ready for the first five questions. The first five questions are all about the United States of Amercia. Question 1 … who was the first President of the United States of America?
(Buzz)
Quizmaster Shirley?
Shirley George Washington.
Quizmaster Correct. Question 2 … when did he become president?
(Ring)
Quizmaster Michael?
Michael 1783.
Quizmaster No.
(Hoot)
Quizmaster Christine?
Christine 1786?
Quizmaster No.
(Buzz)
Quizmaster Shirley?
Shirley 1789.
Quizmaster Correct. Question 3 … in which year did the American Civil War end?
(Buzz)
Quizmaster Shirley?
Shirley 1861.
Quizmaster No-oo.
(Hoot)
Quizmaster Christine?
Christine 1865.
Quizmaster Correct. The Civil War *started* in 1861, Shirley.Question 4 … where was President John Kennedy assassinated?
(Ring)
Quizmaster Michael?
Michael Dallas, Texas.
Quizmaster Correct. Question 5 … who was the first person to set foot on the moon?
(Buzz)
Quizmaster Shirley?
Shirley John Glenn.
Quizmaster No.
(Ring)
Quizmaster Michael?
Michael Buzz Aldrin.
Quizmaster No, he was the *second.*
(Hoot)
Quizmaster Christine?
Christine Neil Armstrong.
Quizmaster Correct, on July 21st, 1969. Now … the next five questions are all about Europe. Fingers on the buttons and here we go. Question 6 … where was Napoleon Bonaparte born?
(Ring)
Quizmaster Michael?
Michael Corsica.
Quizmaster Correct. Question 7 … when did he become Emperor of France?
(Ring)
Quizmaster Michael?
Michael 1769?

Quizmaster No, he was *born* in 1769.
(Hoot)
Quizmaster Christine?
Christine 1804?
Quizmaster No.
(Buzz)
Quizmaster Shirley?
Shirley 1805.
Quizmaster Correct. Question 8 … why was Giuseppe Garibaldi famous?
(Buzz)
Quizmaster Shirley?
Shirley He wanted to unify Italy.
Quizmaster Correct. Question 9 … what is the name of Karl Marx's most famous book?
(Ring)
Quizmaster Michael?
Michael *Das Kapital.*
Quizmaster Correct. Question 10 … where was Karl Marx born?
(Ring)
Quizmaster Michael?
Michael In Russia.
Quizmaster No!
(Hoot)
Quizmaster Christine?
Christine In Germany.
Quizmaster Yes, but where?
Christine I don't know.
(Buzz)
Quizmaster Shirley?
Shirley In Trier
Quizmaster Yes, well done!
(Studio applause)
Quizmaster Now … the next five questions are all about the Far East and Asia. Question 11 … who was the leader of the independence movement during the 1930s and 1940s in India?
(Hoot)
Quizmaster Christine?
Christine Mahatma Gandhi.
Quizmaster Correct. Question 12 … what event caused the United States of America to enter World War Two?
(Buzz)
Quizmaster Shirley?
Shirley The attack on Pearl Harbor.
Quizmaster Correct. Question 13 … when did that take place?
(Buzz)
Quizmaster Shirley?
Shirley December 7th, 1941.
Quizmaster Well done, correct. Question 14 … name the Chinese revolutionary who led the Long March?
(Ring)
Quizmaster Michael?
Michael Mao Tse-Tung.
Quizmaster Correct. Question 15 … when did the Long March begin?
(Ring)
Quizmaster Michael?
Michael 1930.
Quizmaster No.
(Hoot)
Quizmaster Christine?
Christine 1939?
Quizmaster No.
(Buzz)
Quizmaster Shirley?
Shirley 1931?
Quizmaster No, you're all wrong. It started in 1934. Right, that's the end of the first part of the quiz, let's have a look at the scores …
Quizmaster And now we come to the second part of the quiz. I'm going to ask you the listeners questions about seven famous people from the past. Here are the questions:
Question 1: Why is Sir Edmund Hilary famous?
Question 2: Who was Count Leo Tolstoy?
Question 3: What did Alexander Graham Bell do?
Question 4: Who was Marie Antoinette?
Question 5: What is unique about the French physicist Marie Curie?
Question 6: Why did King Edward VIII of England abdicate in 1938?
Question 7: Which Latin American revolutionary fought for the independence of Venezuela,Peru and Bolivia?
Well, that's the end of the questions for this week. We hope you join us on the *History Quiz* next week. Until then, goodbye.
(Studio applause)

Unit 7

● LISTENING 1

Interviewer Why do you think an organisation like the Samaritans is necessary?
Helen I think we live in a society that moves very quickly and often doesn't find a lot of time for people who can't match up to the pressures … that are put on them. It's there for people who are without support at a particularly stressful time and it's often there for people who do have support and do have friends they could talk to but it's something very private that they'd rather take elsewhere, take to someone objective. So the service offers something which is always there … it's befriending without questioning or criticism, it's completely confidential, you'll find a warm response on the phone, someone there to listen to whatever you need to say, whatever the problem is. They won't be shocked or horrified or bored, they'll be there and you'll have their full attention and care and I think it's just something that we don't always find when we need it…
Interviewer What kind of people call the Samaritans?
Helen All kinds of people. Anyone who's lonely or depressed or perhaps just on their own. It could be an elderly lady perhaps who's widowed and has no one in her life to talk to or perhaps a young man who's unemployed.
Interviewer Why did you become a Samaritan?
Helen I wanted to find a way that I could help just with my time and my ability to listen in a way that could possibly benefit others. Um … I just thought about what I was good at, I thought I'm well I'm a good listener, I'm level-headed, I'm not shocked easily perhaps and and I feel I'm probably quite compassionate.
Interviewer This is voluntary work. How much time a week do you spend doing it?
Helen I spend a few hours each week and then once a month we do an overnight shift just to make sure that the phones are manned twenty-four hours a day so people know they can call any time and if they can get through, they will find someone there. Very often the lines are so busy that people have to try again.
Interviewer When someone calls you, do you tell them who you are and do they ask for you when they call again?
Helen We tell people who we are just our first name but we don't encourage them to ask for us by name because it could be very disappointing for them if they were to ring again so we try and encourage them just to speak to anyone who might be there and we usually find that works very well.
Interviewer Is the Samaritans an international organisation?
Helen There are about a hundred branches of the Samaritans worldwide, they don't usually go under that name for various reasons er for example there's a centre in Moscow called the Crisis Centre which offers exactly the same kind of support, a twenty-four hour a day telephone line … .
Interviewer And if people wanted to become a Samaritan, what would they do?
Helen They would contact their local branch, just ring or write in and ask about the organisation and how they could join, then they then would be invited to a meeting where they could learn more about it and take it from there.
Interviewer Is there any training?
Helen There are classes that you attend and they're to assess your ability and just your aptitude for the kind of work. You may well learn in that time that you're not quite sure that you want to do it yourself.

● LISTENING 2

Announcer And now some local news. The village of Millbrook, which is about thirty miles south of Bristol, is not somewhere that you immediately associate with the arts. There are no cinemas or theatres there, and no auditorium where you could put on a concert. But there *is* a big new conference centre and one local resident has decided that he would like to organise an arts festival there. Sarah Thompson went to see how he was getting on.
Sarah Millbrook has three thousand inhabitants, two churches, three pubs, a restaurant and a large conference centre which opened about two years ago.Some of the villagers were a bit put out by the conference centre, which has led to a big increase in traffic through the village. One particular resident, however, has decided that the conference centre presents the village with a golden opportunity. The resident is Mr Rupert Field. Mr Field, what gave you the idea of holding an arts festival at the conference centre?
Field Well … as soon as I saw the new gardens that they had designed, I knew it would be the perfect setting for all sorts of artistic events.
Sarah The gardens … .
Field Yes. There's a nice slope going down to the lake.

Sarah What's the advantage of a slope?
Field It means you can build a stage at the bottom and everyone can see what's going on.
Sarah So ... is that what you're planning to do?
Field Yes. We're going to build a stage at the edge of the lake and invite all sorts of theatres and orchestras, cabaret acts and folk musicians to appear there.
Sarah You're planning to invite some big names, aren't you?
Field Yes. I intend to invite the London Symphony Orchestra, the Royal Shakespeare Company and a number of television celebrities.
Sarah Television celebrities?
Field Yes.
Sarah Can you give us a few names?
Field Not at the moment, no. I want to make sure they're coming first.
Sarah You're going to invite the Royal Shakespeare Company to attend, aren't you?
Field Yes.
Sarah You don't really expect them to accept, do you?
Field Not the main company, no. But they have a touring company, and I've invited them to come.
Sarah And the London Symphony Orchestra?
Field I've invited all of them.
Sarah Won't that cost a lot of money?
Field Yes. And I intend to sell a lot of tickets for the concert.
Sarah With everyone sitting on the grass?
Field Yes
Sarah What if it rains?
Field It doesn't rain much in Millbrook.
Sarah But what are your plans if it does?
Field Well ... we're going to put up a big marquee next to the stage. We'll put the orchestra in there if it rains.
Sarah And what will you do if you don't sell many tickets?
Field I'm hoping to find a sponsor.
Sarah A sponsor ... .
Field Yes. A big commercial operation.
Sarah Have you any idea who that will be?
Field Not at the moment, no. But I aim to find one before the festival starts.
Sarah How much money do you intend to ask the sponsor for?
Field I haven't worked that out yet.
Sarah How many people are you planning to attract to the festival?
Field Oh, at least a thousand. And we intend to make it so interesting that they'll want to stay in the village for a week.
Sarah Where are they all going to stay?
Field We're organising accommodation with local people.
Sarah So ... anyone who attends the festival can stay in the village,
Field That's right.
Sarah And will the villagers put the visitors up, do you think?
Field The ones I've spoken to are very keen.
Sarah How many have you spoken to?
Field About a dozen.
Sarah Is that all?
Field Well, I plan to talk to all of them eventually, starting at church on Sunday.
Sarah Do you think the arts festival will change Millbrook?
Field Oh no. When it's all over, we'll carry on living our lives as if nothing had happened.

Exam practice: paper 4

FIRST PART

Person A Can you give us some idea of the team for Saturday, Brian?
Manager Well, it's very much the same as the team that played against Cardiff last week. Jim Bagley is injured so he won't be playing.
Person B Who'll be wearing Number Four?
Manager Bill Bradley.
Person C So ... Bradley in place of Bagley ...
Manager That's right. Bill's in defence alongside Hunt, Smith and Bagley.
Person A I thought you said Bagley was injured.
Manager Sorry! Yes, you're right. Jim Bagley won't be fit by then.
Person C So, who's in defence?
Manager Hunt,Smith, Bradley and Racket.
Person A What about the midfield?
Manager The same two as last week.
Person B Who was that?
Person A Cross and Purvis.
Person C No, Cross and Barton.
Person A No! Cross and Purvis!
Person C Was it?
Person A Yes!
Manager Terry Barton isn't playing next week.
Person C Why not?
Manager I'm dropping him. Eddie Burton's playing in his place.
Person B So ... Burton instead of Barton. Same number?
Manager Yes.
Person B And Burton's playing in midfield?
Manager No ... in attack.
Person B So who's playing in midfield?
Person A Cross and Purvis!!!
Person C So who's in attack, then?
Manager The two substitutes from last week will link up with Ted Matthews and Steve Henry.
Person B What about substitutes for this week then, Brian?
Manager Barton and Higgins. Right, well, thanks a lot, lads, we've got to get going.

SECOND PART

Hello, this is 099-8877. I'm sorry I'm not here to take your call. please leave a message after you hear the bleep.
(Bleep)

Hello, Gary, hello, this is Angela. I was wondering if you would like to come to dinner on Friday. Call me back.Bye.
(Bleep)

Er ... Hello Mr Davies. This is Eric Brooks from Brooks Art Gallery in Chelsea. We'd very much like you to attend an exhibition of paintings by Welsh artists on Thursday evening. Perhaps you could let us know if you would like to attend? Thank you.
(Bleep)

Gary, it's Paul. How about a game of squash on Friday evening, about six o'clock? Call me back when you get in.
(Bleep)

Hallo, Gareth, this is your mother. Your father and I would like to come and see you. We thought we'd come to your place on Sunday afternoon. Is that all right? Lots of love. Bye!
(Bleep)

Hi, Gary, this is Jonathan. You know mum wants to see you, don't you? Sunday afternoon. I'll come over to your place for lunch first. OK, see you.
(Bleep)

Hallo,Gary, it's Paul again. Can't make it on Friday so I was wondering if we could have a game on Thursday evening, instead? Bye.
(Bleep)

Gary? It's Mr Shilton here. Where have you been today? I want to see you on Thursday afternoon at 4 pm. You'd better be here on time.
(Bleep)

Gary, this is Edith. We've got choir practice on Thursday at four o'clock. Can you come?

THIRD PART

Garton City Council currently spends thirty-four million pounds on local services. Next year, we intend to cut our public expenditure by ten per cent. With this in mind, the following changes are planned:

We currently spend twelve million pounds per annum on local education and we have no intention of changing this. This figure will remain the same.

The amount of money we spend on housing, however, will have to be reduced. At the moment, it's six million pounds. We plan to spend half this amount from public funds in the coming year. This does not mean that our housing service will be reduced in any way. We intend to sell twenty-five per cent of the housing that we own in the city to finance our future housing service.

At the moment, we spend three million pounds annually on the police. We have been told that we must spend more than this next year so the police budget will be increased by one million pounds. we intend to finance this increase by reducing our spending on leisure and recreation by one million pounds.

Spending on Social Services, currently four million pounds, will also be reduced by one million pounds. Our spending on street lighting and cleaning and our budget for ethnic minorities will remain the same.

Administration costs have risen dramatically in the past year, so next year's budget will have to rise. Next year's administration budget will be increased by one million pounds.

FOURTH PART

Sylvia I'm talking to Alan Dibble, the round-the-world cyclist. Hello, Alan, and welcome to the programme.
Alan Thank you, Sylvia. It's very nice to be here.
Sylvia Is it true that you intend to ride a bicycle all the way round the world?
Alan Well ... I'll have to take the occasional plane here and there, but yes, that is my intention.
Sylvia Why are you doing it?
Alan I'm hoping to raise some money for the local hospital here.
Sylvia OK. Tell us something about the route that you intend to take.
Alan First of all, I'm going to ride from Edinburgh to London, and I'm

planning to do a few more radio and TV interviews there to get some publicity. I'm hoping that the TV cameras will be there when I actually set off from outside the Houses of Parliament.

Sylvia Do you think the Prime Minister will be there to see you off?

Alan I hope so. I've sent an invitation, but I've heard nothing yet. So … I'll cycle to Dover, of course, and take the hovercraft to France, and then I've got a pretty long run all the way to Athens.

Sylvia In Greece.

Alan Yes.

Sylvia Then what?

Alan From Greece, I'm taking a boat to Alexandria, in Egypt,and from there I'll cycle down through Saudi Arabia to the United Arab Emirates.

Sylvia Have you ever done anything like this before?

Alan Yes. I cycled across Canada two years ago … that was nearly 5,000 kilometres. There are a lot of Scots in the east of Canada, so I had a big welcome when I arrived.

Sylvia So … where to after the United Arab Emirates?

Alan Well, I plan to stay in Dubai for a couple of weeks for a rest … get a bit of sunshine, you know, and then after that, I'm not absolutely sure what my plans will be. I would really like to get a boat from Dubai to Karachi … .

Sylvia That's in India … .

Alan No, no! Karachi is in Pakistan!

Sylvia Sorry.

Alan And from Karachi, I want to cycle all the way through India to Madras in the south and there I hope to get a boat to Perth in Australia … there's a lot of Scottish people there as well. It's named after a Scottish town, you know.

Sylvia I didn't know. I'm hopeless at geography.

Alan Yes … you must be if you think Karachi's in India! Anyway, after a couple of days staying with my friends in Perth, I'll set off across Australia to Sydney, and then fly to Los Angeles, California. From there it's easy, 4,000 kilometres across the USA to New York and then home from there.

Sylvia I understand you plan to fly back on Concorde.

Alan Yes, I do. There are only two things I have to sort out … one is that Concorde doesn't fly to Scotland.

Sylvia What's the other?

Alan No one has offered to pay for my ticket yet!

Sylvia What is the total distance you expect to cover?

Alan Well, it'll be at least 13,000 miles … that's well over 20,000 kilometres.

Sylvia Well, Alan,everyone here wishes you the very best of luck … .

Alan Thank you … .

Sylvia And I want you to come back on the programme when you get back and tell us what it was like.

Alan I can tell you what it's going be be like now … it'll be very hard!

Unit 8

● LISTENING 1

Good morning, ladies and gentlemen, and welcome aboard Air North flight 601 to Rome and Athens. We shall be taking off in approximately ten minutes' time. I'd like to draw your attention to the safety demonstration that is about to take place …

There are six emergency exits on this plane … two at the front … two in the middle over the wings … and two at the back. If you are instructed to do so by the cabin staff, proceed to the nearest exit as quickly as possible. Do not attempt to take any personal belongings with you, and ladies please remove high- heeled shoes.

The seat-belts on this aircraft are fastened like this … (Click) and unfastened like this … (Click).

There is a life-jacket under your seat. If instructed to do so, put the life-jacket over your head, like this … and tie the straps in a bow at the side. Inflate the life-jacket by pulling the strings. Please do not inflate the life-jacket while you are still inside the plane.

In the unlikely event of a reduction of the air pressure in the cabin, oxygen masks will drop automatically from above your head. If this happens, extinguish all cigarettes, place the mask over your face … like this … and breathe normally.

Please note that smoking is only permitted in the smoking areas. Please do not smoke when the No Smoking sign is switched on … or in the aisles, or in the toilets.

For your information and safety, please read the instruction booklet in the seat pocket in front of you.

Now in preparation for take-off, please make sure your seat-belt is securely fastened, your seat is in the upright position and the table in front of you is folded away.

● LISTENING 2

Gerry Welcome to Talkback Radio, with me, Gerry Sutton. Today we're talking about travel, and the idea is that you ring in with some advice about where to go and what to do, and … more important … what *not* to do. So … I've got Anna from North Wales on the line. Hello, Anna!

Anna Hello, Gerry.

Gerry Welcome to Talkback Radio. Where have you been on holiday, then?

Anna I've just come back from the Seychelles, Gerry.

Gerry The Seychelles!

Anna Yes.

Gerry Did you have a good time?

Anna Wonderful.

Gerry For those people who are listening who don't know … where *are* the Seychelles, Anna?

Anna In the Indian Ocean.

Gerry It must have been expensive to get there.

Anna It was—*very* expensive. But it was worth every penny.

Gerry What advice have you got for any people who might want to go there?

Anna Well, Gerry, we flew from London to the Seychelles, and we didn't have much choice about when we flew.

Gerry Yes?

Anna When we got there, we met some French people, and they told us that there are a lot more flights from Paris to the Seychelles than there are from London. So my advice is to find out how much it costs to fly there from Paris, because it might work out cheaper.

Gerry OK, Anna, what else?

Anna Well, Gerry, I think the most important piece of advice I can give is this: don't book your accommodation with your flight.

Gerry You mean … don't book a package deal?

Anna That's right.

Gerry I thought they were cheaper.

Anna Well, they are in Spain or Portugal, but not in the Seychelles.

Gerry Why not?

Anna Well … if you book accommodation before you go, you may find yourself in a modern hotel. If you just get off the plane and look around, you'll find all sorts of different places to stay … much cheaper and much more intersting.

Gerry OK, Anna, anything else?

Anna Yes. Be careful of the mosquitoes. Take lots of mosquito cream. The holiday brochures don't tell you anything about that.

Gerry Thanks a lot, Anna. So … Anna's advice about the Seychelles: find out about flights from Paris, don't book your accommodation before you leave and take lots of mosquito cream. And now … Tim from Bournemouth. Hello, Tim … hello, Tim?

Tim Hello?

Gerry OK, Tim, you're on the air.

Tim Oh, hello, Gerry.

Gerry What are you going to tell us about, Tim?

Tim Paradors.

Gerry What?

Tim Paradors.

Gerry What are paradors?

Tim Accommodation for tourists in Spain.

Gerry You mean hotels?

Tim No … they're not hotels.

Gerry What are they, then?

Tim They're all sorts of different places … castles, old monasteries … I think there's even one that's an old factory.

Gerry Where are they … on the coast?

Tim No. That's why I'm ringing. My advice is to try a holiday in Spain *away* from the coast. Fly to Madrid instead of Malaga, get a brochure telling you where all the paradors are and hire a car. You'll have the holiday of a lifetime.

Gerry Which parador did you go to?

Tim We went to lots of them.

Gerry Did you book in advance?

Tim No, we just turned up.

Gerry Weren't they full?

Tim Only once.

Gerry What did you do?

Tim We slept in the car. But it was OK, it wasn't cold.

Gerry Well, thanks, Tim. Tim's advice is to forget about a holiday on the beach in Spain and find out about the rest of the country by staying in an old monastery, now called a parador. OK, next on the line is Gill from South London. Hello, Gill!

Gill Hello, Gerry.

Gerry What's your holiday advice?

Gill If you want a holiday in the United States … .

Gerry Yes?

Gill Fly to New York and fly home from Los Angeles.

Gerry And how do you get from New York to Los Angeles?

Gill By car.
Gerry You hire a car ...
Gill No ... don't hire a car. You can get a car for nothing.
Gerry How?
Gill You go to an agency that needs drivers to take cars to other parts of the United States ...
Gerry Yes?
Gill And you tell them you want to take a car to California.
Gerry What kind of cars are they?
Gill Well ... Americans move house all the time, right? They send their furniture by truck and they take the plane.
Gerry Yes?
Gill So they need someone to drive their car.
Gerry I see. And they let someone they don't know drive it.
Gill Yes.
Gerry That sounds a bit dangerous.
Gill No, it isn't. You have to be over 25, you have to have a clean driving licence and you have to leave a deposit.
Gerry How much?
Gill We had to leave five hundred dollars.
Gerry That's a lot of money.
Gill It's only a deposit, you get it back. And you can drive anywhere you like. They gave us ten days to get to Los Angeles.
Gerry What kind of car was it?
Gill A Cadillac!
Gerry Fantastic! So ... Gill's advice if you want a holiday in the United States ... fly to New York and drive someone else's Cadillac to California. Sounds great. Thanks Gill and now ... (Fade)

Unit 9

● LISTENING 1

Interviewer Now, you both keep fit by playing American football. Is that right?
Adam Yeah.
Interviewer Isn't that quite unusual for two English teenagers?
Toby No, not at all. I think there must be at least, I don't know, a few thousand people playing American Football in England now.
Interviewer How did you start?
Adam Well ... I think it's true to say that neither of us was that, you know, interested in sport at school, particularly soccer, which I think is a very boring game. But there was something about American football that looked really exciting.
Toby Yeah. We lived in New York for about six months when we were younger, and we watched a bit of it then. But most people in England are interested because it's been televised a lot in the last few years.
Interviewer So it was easy for you to start ...
Toby Actually, no no it wasn't. There aren't any teams near where we live. We had to travel about twenty miles to find one. And it wasn't easy to get into the team. They make sure that you're really interested before they let you come along to practise. And then you have to wait weeks before they decide if they want you to join.
Adam That's right, but I think they were pretty pleased to see us because we're both quite big and strong, but we also know the rules. They have a lot of difficulty with some of the new players because the rules can be a bit complicated.
Interviewer What sort of thing?
Adam Well, if you're used to playing soccer, I mean, it's a bit of a surprise to find out that you only play for half the game. I mean ... if you're a defence player, you know, you have to come off the field when there's an attacking situation.
Toby Yeah and if you're an attacker, you have to come off the field when the team is playing defence. And Adam is in the attacking line-up and I'm a defence player, so we're not allowed on the field at the same time!
Adam I think the gear is a bit of a surprise to most people, as well.
Interviewer The what?
Adam The gear. The stuff that you have to wear. The helmet and the shoulder pads, all that stuff. It's very heavy and you have to be quite strong just to run around in it, you know.
Toby That's right, and that's why training is so hard. You have to build up a lot of stamina just to wear the gear.
Interviewer What's the training like?
Toby Well, when we start training for the new season, which is in August, September, they make us run around the field dragging a couple of car tyres behind us. It's really hard, especially if you've been on holiday and haven't been keeping fit.
Adam Yeah. Last year, we spent the summer on holiday with mum and dad driving around Canada, and we were in pretty poor condition when we came back. We tried to get out of the first training session, but they wouldn't let us.
Interviewer They wouldn't let you.
Toby Well, they said that if we didn't turn up for training, we wouldn't be allowed to play until after Christmas. So we went, and we had to pull those horrible car-tyres around. It was absolutely impossible.
Adam But it was worth it.
Toby Yeah.
Interviewer Is it a dangerous sport?
Adam Well ... what can you say? People always say you're in much greater danger crossing the road than playing a rough sport, but I suppose it is a bit dangerous. In our last game, one of the other team broke his leg.
Interviewer Really?
Adam Yeah, but he was really, really unlucky. I don't think it's dangerous at all, and you do have to wear all the protective stuff.
Interviewer What do your parents think about it? Did they try to stop you doing it?
Toby Oh no, not at all. But I do think that mum got a bit worried about it.
Adam Yeah, but that was before she came along to see us play. She loves it now, and she wants to learn the rules to understand it better.
Interviewer What about your father?
Adam Well, I think dad's just disappointed that there were no American football teams around when he was a bit younger. I think he's sad that he can't play as well.
Toby Yeah.

● LISTENING 2

Brenda So what's *your* advice to people who want to diet?
Alan I think that the most important thing to tell people who want to lose weight is this: you've got to eat less. There is simply no other way.
Brenda I don't agree.
Alan Listen, Brenda ... most people who are overweight eat too much. The sensible thing to tell them is that they've got to cut down on what they eat.
Brenda No, I'm sorry, Alan, you're quite wrong. People should eat a balanced diet of good food.
Alan Yes?
Brenda It isn't necessary to eat less, it's simply necessary to eat well. Don't eat fast food, eat lots of salads and fresh vegetables and reduce the amount of fried food that you eat.
Alan But that isn't enough. If people think they can eat as much as they like, they'll eat too much, and they won't lose weight.
Linda So basically Alan says that people should eat less ...
Alan Yes.
Linda And you, Brenda, you say that people can eat as much as they like, as long as the food is good ...
Brenda Yes.
Linda Well, I think you're both wrong. Whether you want to eat a healthy diet or lose weight, the important thing is to avoid eating foods that fight.
Brenda I beg your pardon, Linda?
Linda Don't eat foods that fight.
Brenda Foods that fight? What does that mean?
Alan I've heard of that. It's the Hay Diet, isn't it?
Linda Yes.
Alan It's nonsense.
Linda It isn't nonsense, Alan, it works.
Brenda I still don't understand what it means.
Linda The Hay Diet works like this. There are certain types of food which react badly with each other, and should never be eaten at the same time. In fact, they shouldn't even be consumed on the same day.
Brenda What kind of foods?
Linda Well, according to Doctor Hay ...
Alan ... who wrote this rubbish in 1935 ...
Linda ... according to Doctor Hay, proteins and carbohydrates are foods that fight.
Brenda So they mustn't be taken at the same time?
Linda That's right.
Brenda In other words, you mustn't eat meat and potatoes at the same time.
Linda Yes.
Alan Or bread and cheese. It's ridiculous.
Brenda But you can eat ... meat and cheese at the same time.
Linda Yes, because they're both sources of protein.
Brenda So you can eat a cheeseburger.
Linda Yes. But you mustn't eat it in a bun, because bread is a carbohydrate.
Brenda So can you eat different carbohydrates at the same time as well?
Linda Yes.
Brenda Like ... potatoes and pasta?
Linda Yes.

Brenda But they're both fattening foods.
Linda Only if you eat them with the wrong things. You only gain weight if you eat potatoes with butter, or potatoes cooked in fat.
Alan It's no good. You give the impression that people can eat as much as they like and not get fat. I admit that for some people this is possible. Most people need to follow some very clear rules.
Linda For example?
Alan Number one, prepare less food. Number two, take smaller helpings. Number three, don't take seconds.
Brenda But it makes no difference at all if the food isn't good food.
Linda And it makes no difference if you're eating foods that fight.
Alan Look! Once and for all, let's forget this Hay Diet nonsense. I mean ... look at me. I eat bread and cheese nearly every day ... and I'm not fat.
Linda No, you aren't. But there's another reason why you should follow the diet.
Alan What? How can the Hay Diet possibly help someone like me?
Linda If you didn't eat foods that fight ...
Alan Yes?
Linda You wouldn't lose your temper so quickly.

Exam practice: paper 4

FIRST PART

And now some information about school holidays. The school is organising four different visits this year. In February, we are planning a skiing visit to Italy for second and third year pupils. It will last for two weeks and cost £240. Anyone wishing to go on this holiday must give their names to the Deputy Head by 28th November and a deposit of £25 must be paid by Christmas.

At Easter, we are planning a sightseeing visit to Seville in the south of Spain. It is very important that any pupils wishing to take part in this trip inform the school secretary by October 15th at the latest. Seville is very popular at Easter and flights must be booked by November. The cost is £200, which includes tours of the city and surrounding areas. A deposit of £25 must be paid by October 31st.

Our third visit is also at Easter and is for sixth-formers only. We are planning a trip to the city of Boston in the USA. Anyone wishing to make this journey must agree to do a project on family life in New England, which is the part of America where Boston is situated. The flights are at a specially-reduced rate, only £210 per child, with a deposit of £50 payable by January 30th. Those interested must inform the Head of Sixth Form by Christmas.

Our last visit is for first-year pupils and is a climbing holiday in Switzerland. It is scheduled for May and you must let Mrs Jones know by February 1st if you want to go. It costs £70 and we need a deposit by the end of February.

There are sixty places available for the visit to Seville and sixty for the skiing trip. There are, I'm afraid, only sixteen places available for the visit to America and fifty for the climbing holiday.

SECOND PART

Hello, this is World Holiday Transport. Here is some information about charter flights to the USA and Canada this summer. We have flights from Edinburgh to the following destinations: New York, Miami, Los Angeles or Vancouver. Flights to New York or Miami are the same fare. Flights to Los Angeles or Vancouver are in all cases £50 more than the fares quoted to New York or Miami.

First of all, fares to New York or Miami. If you can leave Edinburgh before June 15th, the fare to New York or Miami is £249, but you must return before June 29th. If you wish to return after June 28th but before July 11th, you can do so for only £20 more, for a fare of £269. If you wish to return between July 11th and August 16th, the fare is increased by another £20.

Fares to Los Angeles or Vancouver, leaving before June 15th and returning during the stated periods, are £299, £319, and £339.

The second fare period for all destinations is for flights leaving after June 14th but before June 28th. It is not permissible to return by June 28th on any of these flights, and so there are no fares quoted for this period. Returning before July 11th, the fare to New York or Miami is £299, and £20 more if the return flight is made between July 11th and August 16th.

Between June 28th and August 2nd, you can fly to New York or Miami, returning by August 16th, for £399.

Please note that you must spend at least fourteen days in North America to qualify for these bargain fares.

THIRD PART

Interviewer Norah, you're an actress, aren't you?
Norah Yes.
Interviewer What do you have to do to become an actress?
Norah Well, the simple answer is to say that you've got to go to drama school, but there are a lot of actors who have never studied acting. I went to drama school.
Interviewer Did you enjoy it?
Norah Well, yes and no. It was very exciting. But then, there were some things that we had to do that I thought were a bit stupid.
Interviewer Like what?
Norah Well, one of the teachers insisted that we dressed in the style of a different kind of person every week.
Interviewer What kind of person?
Norah Well, one week we had to dress like an office worker, the next week like a factory worker, then an executive.
Interviewer Did everyone dress the same way?
Norah Oh no! We all had to be different people. So the week that I had to dress like a factory worker, my boyfriend had to dress like an executive.
Interviewer Why did the teacher insist on that?
Norah She said that the only way you could understand what it felt like to be another person was to live like that person. We had to talk to anyone we met in the style of that person, as well. It was very difficult for friends who weren't at the school. They thought we were all mad.
Interviewer But you didn't think it was a good idea?
Norah I thought it was a brilliant idea. The problem was that none of us had the right clothes to play those roles, and we didn't have any money to hire or rent them.
Interviewer And when you left drama school, was it easy to get a job?
Norah No, it's really difficult to get your first job.
Interviewer Why's that?
Norah Well, to get a good acting job, you need an Equity card.
Interviewer You need to belong to the actors' union.
Norah That's right. But you can't get an Equity card until you get a job.
Interviewer So it's impossible.
Norah Not impossible, no. There are some theatre companies that are permitted to give a couple of Equity cards to new actors and actresses every year. Or you can get a series of Equity contracts and work your way gradually to getting one.
Interviewer Have you got an Equity card?
Norah Yes, I have.
Interviewer How did you get it?
Norah I worked as a cabaret singer for a year, and I collected enough contracts to qualify for a card.
Interviewer Do you think the system is a good one?
Norah Oh yes. It stops theatre directors giving jobs to their friends, or someone they want to employ who has never trained or had any experience.
Interviewer So you think every actor should train at drama school?
Norah No, I don't think that. But I think an actor must be very dedicated and professional, and people who want to work hard and make a career in the theatre should have a chance to get a job. That's why the Equity card system is important.
Interviewer So you're happy that you chose to be an actress.
Norah Very happy, yes. You have to work hard and you have to live on very little money, but it's worth it.

FOURTH PART

The idea of using guide dogs to help blind people originated in Germany in the 1920s. This research came to the attention of an American, Mrs Dorothy Eustis, who was training army and police dogs at her kennels in Switzerland. She was very impressed by what she saw in Germany and wrote about it in an American newspaper. The article aroused considerable interest and Mrs Eustis agreed to train a dog for a blind American, Morris Frank. Mr Frank returned to America with his dog.

Mrs Eustis set up a guide dog centre in Switzerland call L'Oeil Qui Voit (The Seeing Eye). In America, guide dogs are still referred to as Seeing Eye Dogs. Guide dog training in Britain began in 1931.

Training a guide dog is expensive, difficult and time-consuming. Dogs need nine months' training at special centres. They must be taught how to walk in a straight line, avoiding any obstacles that occur. It is essential that they learn not to turn corners unless instructed to do so. They must also learn to stop at kerbs and wait for the command to cross the road, or turn left or right. Before working with a blind person, a guide dog must also learn to judge height and width. The dog has to indicate to the blind person when a space is too low or too narrow to pass through safely. Most important of all, the dog must become accustomed to traffic.

Blind people also need four weeks' training at a Guide Dog Centre before they are allowed on the streets with their dogs. They must learn the skills necessary to anyone who works with highly-trained animals ... how to encourage and control the animals effectively.

Even with the best guide dog in the world, a blind person may still need help. If you think that help is needed, always ask first, then let the blind person take your arm when crossing the road.

Unit 10

LISTENING 1

A

Ken What percentage of Japanese marriages are arranged?

Masai It all depend where. Like my home town, it's called Nishio, probably have sixty per cent of Omiai marriages and they're all successful.

Ken How do you know they're all successful?

Masai Well, they haven't got divorced yet!

Ken And what exactly happens with an arranged marriage?

Masai Somebody who introduces this two people um that might be called go-between and they have to exchange their photographs and CVs and family backgrounds and educational backgrounds all that things and then decide whether they like to meet or make appointment … dating and the three of them probably meet … sometimes with the parents as well. They might go to restaurant, have a meal …

Ken So the go-between and the two people who may want to get married meet at the same time …

Masai Yes.

Ken And … so imagine they've exchanged photographs, they've exchanged their CVs and their educational backgrounds … what do they talk about in the restaurant?

Masai Well, they can talk about hobbies and their opinions about things and people, politics and history … so many things they like to talk about, probably yes and then decide … they don't have to decide on the spot, of course, they probably have dating, maybe three months trial and then decide afterwards.

Ken So, I see, so it isn't absolutely necessary for the boy or the girl to marry the person they're first introduced to.

Masai Oh, not at all. I mean … they have quite freedom … lots of freedom to choose and quite often they probably have arranged marriage maybe twenty times and they can still … they can't still find anybody.

Ken Is that common to have … to meet twenty possible marriage partners?

Masai Oh yes, I mean, you never know who it's going to be, you have to feel, you have to really fall in love with somebody. But it's not always the case. It's difficult.

Ken What happens if, for example, the boy falls in love with the girl but the girl doesn't fall in love with the boy?

Masai Oh, that's easy. She can say no through go-between.

Ken Do you think her parents would put pressure on her if er she said no?

Masai Well I think it depends on the family again. If it's a wealthy family, maybe it's a lot of pressure on her, also maybe when she's quite old, they probably worry about her.

B

Are My grandmother was the oldest sister of … I think there were three of them and at that that that time that was end of last last century girls couldn't get married until you know the the older ones had been married and she she was rather choosy and couldn't find a husband and then the other girls said oh we want to get married and … you are not married as yet and she said all right … next man comes, I'll accept her … him. And of course I mean that story went round the village and a man came whom she really hated and asked for her hand and she had promised and they got married. The didn't have a very big wedding as far as I have heard and after six months she was so fed up with the husband she said she was going to get a divorce and of course that time to get a divorce in Estonia that must have been 1860s, but she she she got a divorce and married my grandfather who was a forester and they had two daughters, my mother and her sister and then my grandfather being a forester in Alodaguza, which is a really big forest and he went to the forest and a bear had woken up during the hibernation time and he had a real fight with the bear and was was injured and apparently fainted and was lying in the snow for a long time and got pneumonia and died. When my mother was three, I think.

LISTENING 2

Ann More than thirty per cent of marriages in the United Kingdom end in divorce, the highest rate of any country in Europe. There are also more people who are separated from their husbands and wives than anywhere else. In addition, there are more people in the UK who live together without getting married than in any other country that keeps records of this kind. We asked a marriage counsellor if she could explain these figures.

Interviewer Why are there so many divorces in Britain?

Counsellor Well, first and foremost, it's not difficult to get a divorce. All you have to do is prove that there has been an irretrievable breakdown of the marriage.

Interviewer What does that mean?

Counsellor It can mean almost anything. If a woman has been subjected to violence from her husband, then there's no doubt that there are grounds for divorce. On the other hand, people sometimes feel that there is no benefit in being married to someone that they don't talk to, so they apply for a legal separation.

Interviewer On what grounds?

Counsellor That the marriage isn't working.

Interviewer Isn't getting a divorce an expensive business?

Counsellor The legal costs can be quite high, but a lot of people apply for Legal Aid … .

Interviewer Free legal help … .

Counsellor Yes … which means that they don't have to pay *anything* for legal representation.

Interviewer Has it always been easy to get a divorce in Britain?

Counsellor Not at all. Until 1971, you had to prove that there had been a matrimonial offence.

Interviewer Meaning what?

Counsellor Well, adultery, obviously, and also bigamy. But a prolonged separation would count as well.

Interviewer Do you think that people apply for divorces too quickly nowadays, when things aren't going very well?

Counsellor Not at all. Quite the opposite in many cases. There are a lot of women who are subjected to violence at home who never even tell their family or friends about it.

Interviewer Why don't women who are suffering tell anybody aboutit?

Counsellor Usually because they're frightened. And the terrible thing is that friends and neighbours don't get involved. They often wait for the sufferer to say something first.

Interviewer Are divorces more common in certain areas?

Counsellor Yes. There are many more in big cities, and hardly any in very small towns and villages.

Interviewer Is that because people are happier in smaller towns?

Counsellor Absolutely not! That's not the reason at all.

Interviewer Why are there fewer divorces in small towns, then?

Counsellor Because people are more aware of the people who live in the same community.

Interviewer And this supports people in times of crisis?

Counsellor No. It means that people worry about what their friends and neighbours will say … there's still a great stigma attached to divorce in some areas.

Interviewer Doesn't this happen in big cities as well?

Counsellor Yes, of course it happens everywhere. The difference is that in a city, you're more likely to know people who are divorced or separated. And if you see people making a success of their lives after a divorce, it may encourage you to bring to an end an unsuccessful relationship.

Interviewer So … the main reason why there are so many divorces is that it's easy to get one.

Counsellor I think so, yes.

Interviewer But that doesn't explain why people want to get a divorce. Why do so many people *want* a divorce?

Counsellor Everyone's story is different, and the reasons are usually pretty complex. But I think there are three main reasons. The first is unquestionably this: a lot of people get married when they're too young, If you get married at seventeen or eighteen you're taking a very big risk.

Interviewer Why is getting married in your teens so risky?

Counsellor Because everybody changes so much between seventeen and, say, twenty-three or twenty-four. You're not the same person. And the person you marry isn't, either. Suddenly, you find yourself living with an absolute stranger.

Interviewer And the second reason?

Counsellor Frustration, disaffection … when things aren't going well in your life. Men in particular react very badly if they have problems about money or work. They blame their wives, when that's the very person they should try to share their problems with.

Interviewer And what's the third reason?

Counsellor Meeting someone else and deciding that you'd rather be married to them.

Interviewer Are second marriages more successful than first marriages?

Counsellor No. Just as many second marriages end in divorce. About thirty per cent.

Unit 11

LISTENING 1

Gerry and now here on Talkback Radio, the time is fast approaching 8.30 and that means it's time for … (Jingle) Traffic News. And that

means it's time to say good morning to Amy Kern, who's up over London in the Flying Eye. Hi, Amy.
Amy Good morning, Gerry.
Gerry Where are you?
Amy We're crossing the Thames near Westminster Bridge.
Gerry What's the traffic like?
Amy It's absolutely awful, Gerry. Traffic heading in the direction of Central London isn't moving at all. There's heavy congestion everywhere, particularly in Whitehall, Piccadilly and the Strand.
Gerry Sounds bad.
Amy And it's getting worse, Gerry.
Gerry What's causing all the hold-ups, Amy?
Amy There are just too many cars. And the weather's a problem. More people seem to be on the roads in their cars today because of the rain. I would suggest that anyone listening should come in by train or tube.
Gerry Good idea.
Amy I've got one or two particular problems to report as well, Gerry. There are traffic lights out of order in Pall Mall, St James' Street and Trafalgar Square. There are two broken-down buses ... one in the Haymarket, and the other in Charing Cross Road.
Gerry Anything else?
Amy Yes. There are a lot of roadworks that I should tell you about. The worst ones are in Shaftesbury Avenue, Regent Street and Oxford Street.
Gerry Thanks, Amy. Well ... it sounds like a very good day to stay in bed and listen to Talkback Radio. And today we've got ... (Fade)

● LISTENING 2

Item 1
Here is a late newsflash. One and a half million pounds' worth of gold bullion has been stolen from Salford Security Warehouse near Manchester. Police say that the bullion could have been stolen at any time between 5 pm on Friday and 8 am today, Monday, when a check of the security vault was made. At the moment, police have no idea how the robbers got into the vault.

Item 2
Today police arrested a man in connection with the bullion robbery at Salford Security Warehouse, which took place two weeks ago. The man, who has not been named, appeared in court this morning and was charged with robbery. He was remanded in custody for three weeks.

Item 3
The man who was arrested yesterday in connection with the Salford Security Warehouse robbery has been named as Alan Michael Wigton, described as a building contractor. He will appear before Manchester Crown Court in three weeks' time.

Item 4
Alan Michael Wigton, the man accused three weeks ago of the Salford Security Warehouse bullion robbery, appeared before Manchester Crown Court for the first time today. He was accused of stealing one and a half million pounds' worth of gold bullion. He pleaded not guilty. The counsel for the prosecution told the court that some of the gold bullion was found in a garage in Liverpool owned by Wigton one week after the robbery had been discovered.

Item 5
Today, the second day of the Salford Security Warehouse robbery trial, there has been a dramatic condemnation of the conduct of the police who arrested and charged Alan Michael Wigton. Wigton's defence counsel, Jeremy Smith, declared to the court that his client was the victim of a very elaborate plot to divert attention from the real criminals. There was absolutely no proof that Wigton was anywhere near the warehouse at the time of the robbery, said Mr Smith, who then criticised the police for refusing to explain how they discovered that the bullion was hidden in Wigton's garage. Wigton, he said, admitted that the garage was his, but had no idea how the bullion got there. The case will continue tomorrow.

Item 6
After a three-week trial, Alan Michael Wigton was today found guilty of stealing one and a half million pounds' worth of gold bullion from Salford Security Warehouse on July 11th last year. He was sentenced to seven years' imprisonment. Police announced that they had arrested two other men in connection with the robbery, one of whom works at the warehouse where the bullion robbery took place. It was also revealed that the gold bullion that was recovered from Wigton's garage in Liverpool was worth less than ten thousand pounds.

Exam practice: paper 4

FIRST PART

Teacher Hallo, good evening.
Mrs Bewley Good evening.
Teacher And you are ... ?
Mrs Bewley Mrs Bewley. Jennifer's mother.
Teacher Ah, right.
Mrs Bewley I don't understand this report of Jennifer's.
Teacher I see. What don't you understand?
Mrs Bewley Well, first of all ... why are there two different marks for each subject?
Teacher Well ... one is for classwork ... that's the work done during the term ... and the other is for the end of term examination.
Mrs Bewley But they're different.
Teacher Yes. I'm afraid that's because Jennifer works very well in class but seems to get very nervous in exams. That's particularly true of Science and Maths, where she worked very well during the term and got an A for both subjects. And unfortunately, she only got a D for Maths and an E for Science in the exam.
Mrs Bewley I'm more worried about English. Look ... a D and an E. She's very good at English.
Teacher Well, I agree that she's very *attentive*. She got the D for classwork because she didn't read some of the books that she was supposed to read. As a result, she had a few problems in the exam as well. But she did very well in her French and Spanish classwork, getting an A for French and a B for Spanish, and she managed to get a B in both of her language exams. But in History and Geography, it was the same problem. She got an E for both the exams because she seemed to be very anxious about them. But I think a B is a very fair mark for her classwork in both of these subjects.
Mrs Bewley Well, I don't understand. I always tell her she's got to work harder on her homework but all she wants to do is draw pictures.
Teacher And very good they are, too! Look at that ... two As for her Art.

SECOND PART

Here is an announcement. British Rail wish to apologise for the delays on Intercity services from Birmingham New Street this morning. Trains have been delayed because of adverse weather conditions. Here are the estimated departure times for this morning's Intercity services.

The 10.35 train to Liverpool will now leave at 10.45 from Platform 6. The Sheffield Express, which should have left at nine o'clock, will now depart from Platform 4 at 10.05.

The stopping train to Oxford will arrive at Birmingham New Street at 10.05 and depart for Oxford at 10.15 from Platform 2.

The Manchester Intercity Express will arrive on time at 09.45 and will leave for Manchester at 09.50. This train, which was due to depart from Platform 1 will depart from Platform 6.

The departure to Nottingham has been delayed by the late arrival of the train from Liverpool. This will now arrive at 09.50 at Platform 1. This train will depart for Nottingham at approximately 09.55.

The train now arriving at Platform 5 is the 9.05 from Oxford which will depart for Bristol at 9.20.

THIRD PART

Man Excuse me, can you help me?
Woman Certainly, sir. What do you need to know?
Man I'm interested in one of these office telephone systems, but I'm not sure that I understand what all the functions are.
Woman OK. Which one in particular?
Man Well, this machine here ...
Woman A-ha ... the X12 ...
Man It's got something called Call Hold and Transfer. What does that mean?
Woman Well, it means that if you pick up the phone, and you have to transfer it to another extension, you can do that without going back through the switchboard.
Man Hm ... the phone I've got at the moment can do that. What about Intercom? Does that mean the phone call comes through a speaker?
Woman No. This is something quite different from the old fashioned Intercom systems. With intercom, you can talk directly to a number of different colleagues on other extensions ... all at the same time.
Man We're all in the same office anyway.
Woman Ah.
Man What does three-way-call mean?
Woman That means that you can take an incoming call and talk to a colleague on another extension at the same time.
Man Isn't that a bit confusing?
Woman Well, no. Your colleague can talk to the incoming caller as well.
Man Oh, I see. Er ... what's this Reminder Feature?
Woman Ah ... now that's something we're *very* pleased with. If all your extensions are busy, and another caller is trying to get through, a buzzer sounds on all the extensions.

Man Mm … that might annoy whoever you're talking to. What about Call Intercept … what's that?

Woman That means that if you leave your usual extension and can be located at another one, your call will automatically switch to the new extension, without you having to tell the receptionist that you've moved.

Man I see. And what's this Total Call … what does that do?

Woman Well, if the switchboard is closed, after normal office hours for example, an incoming call will ring at every extension.

Man I see. Well, thank you anyway.

FOURTH PART

Commentator And it's Barber to serve.

(tennis serve)

Commentator It's in the net. Serving again.

(tennis serve)

Official Out!

Official Love-forty.

Commentator Well … Barber is giving us a marvellous demonstration of how *not* to serve in a tournament of this importance. Schlagel now has three match points and looks ready to walk straight into the second round. The twenty-three-year-old left-hander from Bristol seems to be staring defeat in the face. He serves again …

(tennis serve)

Commentator … and *again* it's in the net.

Beryl This is the worst serving I've ever seen in a major tournament.

Commentator Barber serving again …

(tennis serve, crowd applause)

Commentator And that's it … two double-faults and he's out of the competition.

Official Game, set and match to Schlagel, 6-4, 7-5, 6-1. Barber loses to Schlagel in straight sets, 6-4,7-5, 6-1.

Beryl We have seen today another demonstration of how poor British tennis is at the moment. Barber was slow, his service lacked variety or pace, his returns of service were predictable or inaccurate, and his overall game seemed completely unsuitable against a German who isn't even very well known in his own country. Barber simply isn't good enough at this level and if he wants to carry on playing, he has to go back to basics immediately.

Commentator And yet he started so well.

Beryl Oh yes, he started well.

Commentator Why do we see so many British players fade like this?

Beryl Well, there are a number of reasons, but the main one in Barber's case is that he doesn't look fit. He looks overweight, he isn't muscular enough and he seems to have no stamina.

Commentator And yet some of the other British players, the ones who *are* fit, they don't seem to fare any better.

Beryl You're quite right, but with the others, I think it's mainly a question of attitude. I don't think most of them prepare themselves by saying 'I'm going to win this match'.

Commentator You think they go out expecting to lose?

Beryl I think they lose confidence at the first sign of trouble.

Commentator Any recommendations for any young players who may be listening?

Beryl Make sure you're in good condition and think about your attitude to the game.

Commentator Thank you Beryl. Oh dear, and it's started raining as well. So, from a very sad and depressing Kings Club … back to the studio.

Unit 12

● LISTENING 1

Reporter And now, a rather strange question. How intelligent is a house? what can a house do? Did I hear you say 'nothing'? Well, you may not think about it very much, but a modern house can do quite a lot. It can provide constant sources of electricity, water and gas and a link with the outside world through a telephone line. In addition, with the help of a few sophisticated gadgets, a house can switch on lights when you aren't home to deter burglars, it can start cooking food before you come home, and take messages from people who telephone while you're out.

Scientists, though, are currently working on sophisticated new technology which will make today's houses seem very old-fashioned indeed. Very soon, we will be able to live in something called The Intelligent House. Scientist Stephen Hall is working on a particular invention for the intelligent house.

Hall Basically … er … today's … a house today doesn't do what people … what *busy* people want it to do … or rather, need it to do. Take … er … security, for example. I mean, a modern house isn't, you know, what you might call protected. All you have is … er … a simple device like a burglar alarm … someone opens the door, the front door and the … the alarm goes off and that's about it, really. I've designed a whole new … a completely new system of burglary prevention. If someone, a burglar, breaks into an intelligent house, a heat-sensitive camera, a mobile camera, will, you know, locate him, the burglar, and his picture will appear at a local crime prevention centre, a police station, in other words. And the burglar will only have to cough and the police will be able to find him on a computer. And the … um … the owner of the house will also carry a little … a little gadget … so he'll be alerted to the danger as well.

Reporter Yes, but what if the burglar is wearing a *mask* or hasn't got a cough? Still, intelligent houses will be able to do more than simply take photographs of intruders. Here's our Science correspondent Clare Thompson.

Thompson By the year 2020, say, the vast majority of city-dwellers will live in intelligent houses and apartments. The'll be able to programme their houses in the same way that people programme their computers. As they leave in the morning … they'll be able to tell their houses when to cook dinner, what to take out of the fridge and so on. The house will even be able to order food and other commodities from shops thanks to a computerised shopping system. In fact, the house will shop around until it gets the best price, order the goods and arrange for them to be delivered … all before the occupant returns home! It'll be possible to programme your house when you aren't even there … even when you're abroad, using a simple progression of codes that the house recognises.

And of course, you'll be able to change your mind. You might programme your house to cook a meal for four people, and then you might invite two more people to dinner. You simply call the house and change the order. And if the house hasn't bought enough food, it'll get on the phone and get some more delivered.

Reporter Imagine that! Calling your house and telling it to cook a meal for six people. And what happens if you call the wrong house? Will someone *else* come home and find a huge meal prepared?

● LISTENING 2

And now … *Journey to the End of Space* …

The Space Ship Red Comet is passing through the Andromeda Galaxy with its captain, Jane Blake, at the controls and her alien co-pilot Dark Ardvark at her side. Jane is eating something delicious.

Jane Can I tempt you with one of these delicious cakes, Dark?

Dark No thank you, Captain. I had one about five minutes ago.

Jane I know, it's pure greed that keeps me eating them. Did you know …

Dark Captain Blake!

Jane … I was on a train once and I ate a whole box of these cakes in half an hour …

Dark Captain … this is serious!

Jane No, it wasn't, Dark, I didn't put on any weight at all … not an ounce! I don't know how …

Dark Captain! I am not talking about your eating habits! Look at the screen!

Jane What is it, Dark?

Dark It's the square thing in front of you, Captain.

Jane Dark, I know what a screen is. What is the problem?

Dark We appear to be heading in the direction of an asteroid cloud, Captain.

Jane Hey! That is serious!

Dark We must find a way to avoid the asteroids, Captain. Otherwise, the space ship will be destroyed.

Jane I agree, Dark. The main thing is to avoid the asteroids. I'll talk to the computer. Hallo, Cosmo … Cosmo, can you hear me? Hey, Cosmo! Wake up!

Dark I don't think the computer is working, Captain.

Jane It's OK, Dark, Cosmo is just asleep. COS-MO!

Cosmo Go away. I want to be alone.

Jane COS-MO!!!

Cosmo You have a loud voice, Captain.

Jane For goodness sake, Cosmo! Stop acting the fool. We need your help, and we need it now. We have a serious problem on our hands here.

Cosmo I don't care. You agreed that I could take a rest … if I don't get some sleep, I can't guarantee that I will be in full working order for the rest of the journey.

Jane Let me make this as plain as I can, Cosmo … we are heading in the direction of an asteroid cloud.We could be in very serious trouble if you don't wake up and switch yourself on and come up with a good idea.

Cosmo I understand your problem.

Jane Good.

Cosmo But there is nothing I can do.

Jane What?

Cosmo You promised that I could have a sleep this year. This is the first time I've switched myself off for more than five years. I'm under great strain, Captain, and I'm allowed to take a rest if I have to.

Jane Cosmo! I order you to switch yourself on!

Cosmo You can't make me.

Jane Cosmo, you are such a pain! I'm going to switch you on and work out how to change course myself.

Cosmo Do not attempt to use the computer without my permission. The results could be disastrous. You cannot operate the space ship without my help.

Jane I don't care what you say. I'm going to have a go.

Dark Please be careful, Captain

(Noise of chaos and panic)

Will the Spaceship Red Comet avoid the asteroid cloud? Will Captain Blake learn to use the controls? Will Cosmo the Computer get any sleep tonight? Will Dark Ardvark regret that he did not accept the Captain's offer of a delicious cake? Listen next week to ... *Journey to the End of Space*!

Final exam practice: paper 4

FIRST PART

Interviewer Doctor Bell is an expert on urban traffic problems. Doctor Bell ... you are very pessimistic about the future of traffic in cities, aren't you?

Bell I am indeed. Almost all of the world's major cities are heading for a situation of complete traffic paralysis, where the entire centre of the city is so snarled up that nothing will move for an entire day, perhaps longer. The only major city that I predict will avoid this danger is Moscow, because there simply aren't enough cars there to create the problem.

Interviewer Which cities are in most danger of this traffic paralysis?

Bell New York, Tokyo, Paris and London. Take Paris as an example. At the moment, traffic moves around Paris at an average speed of twelve kilometres an hour. In London, it's a little more ... about fifteen kilometres an hour. Yet in both cities, it is predicted that by the year 2025, the increase in traffic could be as much as 125 per cent ... in other words, more than double the amount of cars that use the cities today.

Interviewer How many cars are we talking about?

Bell In London, two million cars drive into or around the city every day. In thirty years time, this will be four million, according to official government statistics.

Interviewer But surely the majority of these cars are taking people to their place of work?

Bell That is correct, the majority are. But those cars are only carrying fourteen per cent of the workforce. The other eighty-six per cent use public transport or walk or cycle to work. The danger will be that more and more people will choose to go to work in a car rather than by public transport.

Interviewer Why will people choose to do that?

Bell People will choose to travel into the city by car when public transport becomes too expensive, too dirty, too unreliable or too dangerous.

Interviewer But won't people realise that traffic is getting slower and slower, and start taking public transport again?

Bell Maybe. But by that time, the public transport system will have reduced its capacity, if it still exists at all, and it will no longer be possible for these people to travel into the city by that means. But before that happens, before people realise that it is completely stupid to try to drive to work, car-users will have experienced the biggest traffic jam in history. And I will explain how it will take place. It will take just two accidents happening at the same time at important junctions in the centre of the city, at one of the busiest times of the day, and we will find that traffic is unable to move anywhere in the centre. It happened in Los Angeles in 1979, and I predict that it will happen in the 1990s in either Paris or London.

SECOND PART

The Taylor report on sports stadiums makes a lot of predictions about the way we will watch sport in the 21st century. The compilers of the report appear to be in favour of many of the developments that they predict.

Take all-seater stadiums, for example. The report makes it quite clear that there is no better improvement that can be made. All-seater stadiums will reduce the incidence of violence, and make stadiums generally safer.

On the subject of building new stadiums outside towns, there is less certainty. Whilst the new stadiums would be safer and better, the trend towards out-of-town stadiums is not welcomed in the report. They see the need for everyone to have to drive to a sports stadium as a step backwards.

On ground-sharing by local football or other sporting clubs, the report has no doubts. It is an excellent idea and should be encouraged wherever possible. It also makes a series of recommendations about what should be done with the land on which the redundant stadium stands.

The report comes out against the use of wire fences and other barriers to prevent spectators from getting on to the pitch at soccer matches. Whilst the clubs may prefer to see the fans fenced in, there is no doubt that fencing presents a safety risk.

There seems to have been some disagreement amongst the committee that compiled the report on the subject of artificial pitches. There is a great deal of criticism of plastic playing surfaces, especially at soccer grounds, but the report's final decision is that they are vital to the future of sport in the community. They looked forward to a time when every town had at least one plastic pitch for the use of local sports teams and the community.

The committee was unanimous in its belief that new stadiums must not be built with only one sporting activity in mind. Wherever possible, any future stadiums should be built to house as many different sports as possible.

THIRD PART

Brenda With me in the studio is music journalist, Andy Cassidy. Hi, Andy.

Andy Hi, Brenda.

Brenda Andy, you're an expert at predicting new trends in popular music. What are your predictions for the mid 1990s?

Andy Well, I think the success of world music will continue ...

Brenda World music ...

Andy Yes, music which is influenced by styles from all over the world, Africa, Latin America ... that kind of thing. I think we'll see a lot more bands with musicians of many different nationalities.

Brenda How do you mean?

Andy Well, it's not unusual now to see a band with an African percussion player, a Brazilian guitarist and an American saxophone player ... and they probably all live in Paris. I think that kind of thing will continue.

Brenda What about the singers?

Andy Ah ... that's going to be the biggest change of all. At the moment, a lot of world music groups sing in English, even if there are no English-speakers in the band.

Brenda Do they sing in English even if they're performing in non-English speaking countries?

Andy That's right.

Brenda Why is that, do you think?

Andy They still think that's what people want to hear. But I think the Gypsy Kings changed all that.

Brenda The Gypsy Kings. They sing in Spanish, don't they?

Andy Well, they're from France and they sing in a kind of dialect of Spanish. Anyway, they were very succesful. I think more and more people will get the idea that it's better to sing in your own language.

Brenda So ... is this the end for English-speaking groups?

Andy Not at all. But they'll have to compete with singers who speak other languages.

Brenda Any more predictions?

Andy Yes. I think we're going to hear more music from the Far East. There are some Japanese bands who I think will be very famous.

Brenda Andy Cassidy ... thank you for talking to us.

Andy Pleasure.

FOURTH PART

Interviewer Excuse me?

Resident Yes?

Interviewer Would you mind answering a few questions?

Resident Not at all.

Interviewer Are you a resident in this area?

Resident Yes, I am.

Interviewer Can I ask you which party you voted for at the last election?

Resident The Social Democrats.

Interviewer I see. And do you think you'll vote the same way next time?

Resident I don't know.

Interviewer What do you think is the most important local issue?

Resident Well, I'm quite worried about the state of the roads and provisions for old people, but my main concern is education.

Interviewer Education. Have you got any children?

Resident Yes. Two.

Interviewer And ... are they at school?

Resident Not yet.

Interviewer What improvements would you like to see in schools?

Resident Well, it seems to me that not enough money is being spent on education and some of the school buildings are quite old but the most important thing to me is that the classes are too big.

Interviewer I see. That's really helpful. Thank you for your time.